WEEDONOMICS® 101

THE ENTREPRENEUR'S GUIDEBOOK
TO THE CANNABIS INDUSTRY

TODD JOHNSON

HOW TO GET REAL, GET CLEAR, GET EDUCATED AND GET IT DONE

Weedonomics 101: The Entrepreneur's Guidebook to the Cannabis Industry
Published by Enceladus Press
Denver, CO

ISBN: 978-1-7344079-0-7

BUSINESS & SELF HELP / Industries / Agribusiness

Cover and Interior design by Victoria Wolf

Photo by Ralston Photo

Printed in the United States of America.

WEED·O·NOM·ICS (wēd) ə'nämiks/*noun*

plural noun: weed**onomics**

- A social science concerned with the people, production, distribution, and consumption of goods and services in the cannabis industry. We optimize how individuals and businesses interact, satisfying needs and wants to achieve maximum satisfaction for all.

- A path to the creation of favorable or advantageous circumstances.

- A pivot point for personal and professional progress or advancement.

- A chance to change the world for the better.

- An opportunity to uncover your best self.

UNDER PRESSURE

DAVIE BOWIE & QUEEN

Prologue

YOU'VE BEEN THERE ... you're driving along, thinking about random things: issues at work, kids you have to pick up, dinner you have to make, what you are going to do when you get where you are going ... life things. Then you see the flashing lights. You are about to get pulled over. You look down immediately to see how fast you are going, and it's not good. You start thinking about what you are going to say, where you are going to stop, and if you have the documents you need. You feel a rush of stress and anxiety.

I have to admit, I'm a little different. I generally enjoy getting pulled over. I see it as a full-pressure, real-life, on-the-court challenge. There's a very fine line between pushing the envelope and showing genuine respect for the officer, *which I do*, but if you balance it right, you can leave with a reduced ticket, if you get a ticket at all. One year I got pulled over fourteen times (it's possible I speed a little) and escaped with six points instead of a potential forty-two.

However, none of those fourteen stops compared to the day I got pulled over on a felony stop. On that particular day, everyone in passing cars knew this was a situation they didn't want to be in … and neither did I. A felony traffic stop is one where the police think you have committed a felony and treat you as if you are armed and dangerous. If you haven't experienced one, it's scary and chaotic. Full disclosure: this was my second felony stop. The first was a case of mistaken identity where I ended up handcuffed and face-down with guns pointed at me. My lesson from that one was to always follow the officer's directions.

This second felony stop was much different. Though it was only 7:00 a.m., I remember it feeling later as I had been awake since 4:00 a.m. My Dodge diesel pickup was warming up in the driveway, and I invested my nervous jitters in giving it the most thorough inspection I could – turn signals, headlights, tire pressure, examining the windshield for cracks, and making sure the insurance card, registration, and license were in place. I checked for anything and everything that might draw attention to me.

On that crisp morning, the thought of driving thirty miles with over eighteen pounds of marijuana, eighteen times the legal transport amount in Colorado, had me on edge. Everything was sealed and double-wrapped in 3-mil-thick plastic contractor trash bags, taped and zip-tied. Even though it was under a topper in the truck bed, it might as well have been sitting out in the open. With quality and quantity this high, the scent enveloped the inside of the vehicle. If I got stopped for any reason, it was over. *Jail time.*

Growing, selling, and moving marijuana is legal in the state of Colorado, but it is a federally illegal activity. Depending on who pulled me over and what areas were included in the officer's jurisdiction, repercussions could range from nothing to being reported to the DEA. Involving the DEA would be a complete disaster. I had good reason to believe this.

On a Thursday night in February 2010, 9News – a Denver-based NBC affiliate – advertised a forthcoming story about Chris Bartkowicz and his extensive medical marijuana growing operation. He boasted in the ad trailer about his role as a caregiver to a number of medical-marijuana patients, and how his booming business (complete with video footage of his home and neighborhood) was helping him live the dream by turning an annual profit of several hundreds of thousands of dollars. The following morning, his story was again featured by 9News in a website article, and the story was picked up and published by *The Denver Post* that same day. That night, the story aired on television. Very soon after, federal DEA agents converged on Bartkowicz's house, got his permission to search, and seized his operation. He was ultimately convicted of a felony and sentenced to five years in prison.

Now, to be fair to the DEA, Bartkowicz did something even most legal growers in Colorado don't do: he flaunted his success in a significantly public way. When you flaunt your federally illegal activities in a way the DEA can see, you can expect problems. Bartkowicz got them. The DEA does what it's expected to do, and it believes what it is doing is the right thing. The rules are the rules, as they say, but I have seen variability in how those rules are enforced. Testing the DEA in a defiant, arrogant, flaunting way is a recipe for disaster, and I was entering the same realm in a Dodge pickup full of high-grade marijuana.

As I stood in the driveway, my inspection complete, I stalled – not eager to hit the road just yet. I thought of Bartkowicz and wondered, *"How did I get here? What the fuck am I doing? What. The. Fuck. Am. I. Doing?"*

I took a deep breath and envisioned my "girl in the red coat." If you remember the movie *Schindler's List*, one of the most impactful elements in the three-and-a-half-hour, black-and-white movie are the scenes with the little girl in the red coat. Liam Neeson as Schindler is sitting on a horse and watching the chaos and devastation as a ghetto gets liquidated. What makes the scene so amazing is that you are watching an epiphany, an "aha" moment, a moment of clarity, and at the same time, a point of no return – with no dialogue. This child is one of millions, but she touches his soul in a way that transforms his life, the work he is willing to do, and the lives of thousands of others.

My "little girl in a red coat" is a fourteen-month-old baby, although her situation was nowhere near as heavy or devastating as the Holocaust. Her family came to Colorado from a southern state in search of hope and a chance for their daughter to have a great life, like we all want for our children. This baby was nearly catatonic all the time and suffered sixty to seventy seizures a day as a result of Dravet syndrome, a rare genetic version of epilepsy. They came to our dispensary and we used a 32-to-1 CBD to THC oil that was atomized as a spray specifically for her. Her life, and the lives of her parents, were positively changed forever as a result. The number of seizures she suffered reduced to about seven per week, and she became a gregarious and bubbly baby. This drive was worth it.

I knew what I was doing and I believed in the work. I took a deep breath and got in my truck. The longer I waited to make my delivery, the greater the likelihood of traffic, maybe a fender bender, or more police presence on the roads. I needed to get moving.

Usually, I haul my product as mandated by law – no more than a pound at a time, dried and sealed. This haul was particularly wet, sticky, and heavy, and the dispensary I was working for needed it immediately. To make sure the dispensary got it quickly, it had offered to trim and dry it by themselves. This increased my risk since wet and/or unsealed marijuana is easily noticeable, and the plants as a whole are way more pungent. Deliveries are the most nerve-wracking aspect of this business, by far. Depending on how nosy one's neighbors are, most growers are able to keep their grow operations under the radar. Delivery day, however, especially with the variation in state and federal legalities, causes a person to look in the mirror and ask, "How brave am I?" I was pushing the limits, but this entire business pushes the limits. I could just as easily get into trouble with the feds for transporting one pound in a state-safe way. Bumping that up to eighteen pounds minimized the number of trips I'd need to make, which seemed like a good way to mitigate the risks associated with eighteen trips. Like I said, it's all a risk, one that each person in this business weighs out for oneself.

I started driving. Carefully. I was driving, trying to keep cool, and staying a little over the speed limit just to look legit, checking every car for anyone swerving even slightly, letting everyone merge, looking around constantly in every direction, and keeping an eye out for cops. Up ahead, I saw the potential for trouble. A police car sat in an old toll booth station, where cameras are now in use.

I told myself to stay calm. I wasn't speeding and so I rolled right on by. That's when I saw the patrol car move out of its spot, the lights turn on, and the car merge into traffic. My heart dropped.

Before the police car pulled in behind me, I had remained hopeful that it was going elsewhere. That has happened to me before, but it didn't happen that day. I turned on my signal and began to ease over to the side of the road, taking a few deep breaths. I knew it was critical to remain calm. The officer rolled to a stop behind me. He waited for a few agonizingly long moments before exiting the vehicle. They do this sometimes … they wait. I knew he was probably checking my license plate before approaching me.

Finally, he walked up to the truck and the wrinkle in his nose told me he could smell the marijuana contained inside my truck. I rolled down my window, and before he could even give the typical spiel, I said, "Sir, before you say it, I know this doesn't look good. I want to explain what is happening here and it's not as bad as it appears."

"That would be a shock," he replied.

"Yes, you're right," I continued. "But let me tell you. I work as a grower for a dispensary, and I have my card right there. According to the laws in Colorado, I can transport marijuana strictly for business purposes."

"We'll get to that," he said dryly, as if he heard such excuses every day. But it wasn't an excuse, not for me. "For now, let me see your license and registration. And do you have any guns?"

I shook my head no.

"Sit tight," he said, and walked away.

I waited a full ten minutes, which felt like a lifetime. A second police car pulled up, then another, plus two undercover vehicles, and that was when I started to really worry. The officers got together and started talking, hands on holsters and serious looks on their faces. Eventually, they came up on both sides of my truck and asked if they had my permission to search the vehicle.

"Yes, of course," I said.

I was escorted to the back of one of the patrol cars to wait. In case you've never been in the back of one (and I hope you haven't), here's what it's like: a thick panel – plastic on top, metal on the bottom – separates the back seat from the front seat. There are no door locks or door handles. It's tight, and an acrid scent of discomfort oozes from the utilitarian hard plastic seat. I watched as the officers laid out the contents of my truck, making a neat line of bags along the side of the shoulder.

Finally, an officer came up to the car where I was waiting and opened the door and asked me to step out – which I did gladly, though with a good deal of trepidation.

"Mr. Johnson, we aren't sure what to do here legally. There are no guns, as you said. There are also no contraband of any kind, no weed in the ashtray, and no open containers. Your license and insurance are current and your registration is up to date, but you're carrying an incredible amount of marijuana."

"I do have the dispensary patient list book to show you I'm not making this up," I offered. I showed it to him and that seemed to help. They believed me and nothing I demonstrated in my vehicle suggested any reason not to. It was undoubtedly the biggest moment of relief I have experienced.

When I think back to that moment, I often wonder why they let me go. I was carrying over the legal limit, no doubt about it. But they were state officials, not federal officers. And, I had the documentation I needed and the confidence to deliver it. My ducks were in a row – license, registration, insurance, a clean ashtray (I actually don't use marijuana) and no alcohol.

I left the pull-over with a warning that day. No, it wasn't a warning about the amount of marijuana I was hauling. Rather, it was a warning that I needed to consider removing the shaded license plate cover on my truck. The officer was worried about me evading the cameras and tolls on the toll road, and that was why he had pulled me over.

I've added that to my delivery checklist now – *no obscure license plate.*

This story is a real-life example of the heart-racing moments in store for people who enter the marijuana business – although I hope most people's heart-racing moments don't involve felony stops. This industry is edgy, ever-changing, and in need of great businesspeople like you to chart its course. If you are reading this book as a stepping-stone into the marijuana industry, you won't be disappointed … and you will be ready.

However, if you strip the context of the marijuana industry out of this story, you get the story of a passionate person, pushing the limits under extreme stress, in order to accomplish great things. In other words, the story of an entrepreneur.

Marijuana industry entrepreneurship isn't any different from other entrepreneurship: business leaders looking to capitalize on and/or create opportunities in an emerging industry. This is a book for entrepreneurs (current and burgeoning). It is also a leadership book. It is a book about preparing and honing the most critical asset in managing an amazing opportunity, as well as the unthinkable stress of starting and running a business: you.

HELLO IT'S ME

TODD RUNDGREN

The Author and the Book

THIS IS NOT ANOTHER "BUSINESS BOOK" filled with get-rich-quick advice on leveraging the cannabis industry. It is, instead, a book that will inspire you, change your life, alter your perspective on the world around you, and help you find your place in it. If you engage with this book, I believe you'll be set up to become a successful entrepreneur. You'll learn that you can get rich and *sustain* it too! I promise no other book can deliver like this book will – but you have to be willing to fully engage, help me with a few things, and then go play full out.

Weedonomics is going to ask you to **Get Real, Get Clear, Get Educated,** and then **Get It Done.** This is the first book in a two-book series, and it sets you up to lead and run a business (focused on businesses in the marijuana industry). The second book, *Weedonomics Grow Pro*, is a how-to grow book. It is a proven, superior grow system with photos, diagrams, and step-by-step instructions for every aspect of the process. The system is going through the patenting process right now. However, to succeed in any business, you need to **Get Real** with yourself before you put yourself out there financially and emotionally: deal with yourself, know your strengths and weaknesses, and reflect on your experiences to mine for the moments that can change you for the better. Doing this gets you ready to face challenges and lead others through authentic relationships, and it prepares you to survive the tough times any business can face.

Then, you need to **Get Clear** by naming your passion and vision so you have a defined direction and focus. Getting clear also helps you articulate your direction and focus to those you interact with, and this will lead to shared vision building. Next, you have to **Get Educated** and become a master of your domain. There's a lot to running a business (people management, sales, culture, finances, etc.), and you're responsible for knowing all of it. Finally, you need to **Get It Done**: put everything together with fidelity and get to work.

Most entrepreneurs focus solely on the last two stages: getting educated and getting it done. This is one of the main reasons why so many people fail. In any business, just getting educated and getting it done, without getting real and getting clear first, don't prepare you to lead through the unknown and the uncertain – staples of the entrepreneurial world. Most businesspeople, when they face stress, challenges, and adversity ... get overwhelmed and the endeavor folds. One of the only things you can count on in the world of entrepreneurship is yourself: how well do you know yourself? What do you bring to your leadership? What do you rely on in the most trying times?

Everyone's life is made up of a series of moments – good and bad. It's who you are, and your awareness of yourself that carries you across those moments more reliably than any knowledge set. Said more simply, who you are matters more than what you know. Think you're a hard worker and you can just muscle through the tough stuff? Think again. It's *how* you work as a leader *and* that you work hard that determines your outcomes. And when you fail, and you will as a natural part of entrepreneurship, it's your internal compass that will point you in the right direction again.

If you're telling yourself that this sounds like touchy-feely bullshit, you are dead wrong.

It's possible you may be uncomfortable facing yourself. As an entrepreneur, you have to look yourself in the mirror every day because everything depends on you ... I have done it, and no professional experience has been more valuable than the work I've done on myself.

WHO YOU ARE MATTERS MORE THAN WHAT YOU KNOW.

Don't believe me? Here are a few pieces of data to consider:

- According to the article "Hire for Attitude" from *Forbes*, it states, "We tracked 20,000 new hires, 46% of them failed within 18 months. But even more surprising than the failure rate, was that when new hires failed, 89% of the time it was for attitudinal reasons and only 11% of the time for a lack of skill."

- Michal Bloomberg, the fourteenth-richest person in the world with a $40-billion-plus net worth, said in an article about the ideal job candidate: "I've always said I would like to hire a person whose father was never there, whose mother was in a drug treatment program and he had to go to work three shifts [a week] at McDonald's to take care of his siblings. That's the kind of person you want – somebody who, no matter how bad things are, looks on the bright side, takes the bull by the horns, puts in the sweat capital and that's where the results are."

- Warren Buffett offers six pieces of wisdom in an article by Kathleen Elkins on CNBC, all of which touch on this central idea:
  - Marry the right person. (It will make more of a difference in your life than almost anything else.)
  - Invest in yourself. (Learn to communicate better both in writing and in person.)
  - Associate yourself with "high-grade people." (Start acting more like them.)
  - Work for people you respect. (You don't want to take a job just for the money.)
  - Ignore the noise. (Keep a level head and stay the course.)
  - Success isn't measured in money. (Being given unconditional love is the greatest benefit you can ever get.)

I trust this data generated from some of the most successful businesspeople ever. It says nothing about education, how much money you have, how big your house is, or cars or planes you own. It's "Who" before "What."

What you know (information) *is* important, but you can find the answers to almost anything in an instant and understand almost anything if you have the desire and persistence. This book will help you do just that in the Get Educated and Get It Done sections. If you're going to be a successful entrepreneur, you need to understand that what you know and your skills move in an orbit around who you are. Before we get into *the* work, I want you to read three more chapters:

- The first (*Everybody Wants Some!!*) is going to help you connect to the benefits ahead for you in the entrepreneurial world.

- The second (*Stressed Out*) will name the darker side of entrepreneurship and how this book can help you face it, and avoid those pitfalls (or address them, if you are currently living that life).

- The third (*People*) is going to make sure you understand the balance between the personal and the professional in making it as a leader.

Another thing you'll notice about this book is that it does not have traditional titles or "meaningful" quotes to begin each chapter. Honestly, I think that's boring and has been beaten into the ground. Instead, each chapter is a song title. Is there anything that can move your mood or memory more quickly than music? Movies know it. Television shows know it. Advertisers know it. So why not a book?

Each song title ties into the content of its specific chapter, and often the content of the song ties into the messages in the book. Hopefully, this helps you better connect to and engage with the material. I offer many different artists, most pulled out of my own library. Ideally, you could create a playlist that helps you enjoy the book and ties you back to the content. Music has always been an important part of my life, as it has been throughout human history. I was a Jazz DJ at a Denver radio station for many years, so it's kind of in my blood. Maybe you'll hear something new or be reminded of a favorite that moves you to action and helps you remember what you read.

To make it easier, the Table of Contents lists the song titles first and the traditional subtitles underneath to help you find what you need quickly.

Before we really get started, here is a fair warning and where I need your help:

WARNING! Your mission, should you choose to accept it, starting now, is this: this book is going to ask you to be more personal, real, and vulnerable than any business book ever has. Be totally honest about how you feel, what your failures have been, what your short-comings are, who you really are, and what you really want. I have left open spaces that can only be filled by you. By the time you reach the last page, no two books will be the same. That is how integral your reflection is to your success. We are building your skyscraper of success. Keep in mind: no one has ever built anything lasting or impressive without first creating a strong foundation.

If you agree to the terms in the warning, and I have your permission to proceed, please keep reading. Grab a pen or pencil, and let's go!

TABLE OF CONTENTS

PARTS 1 & 2

THE ROOTS

GET REAL: Know Yourself

GET CLEAR: Define Your Vision

GET EDUCATED: The Business - The People

GET EDUCATED: The Opportunity

GET IT DONE

EVERYBODY WANTS SOME!!

VAN HALEN

Entrepreneurship: Why not?

POWER. FREEDOM. CHOICE.

Everybody wants some! And why not? Power, freedom, and choice are three perks that being your own boss offers. These words are used often, probably overused, so let's quickly look at their definitions. **Power:** the ability to do something or act in a particular way. **Freedom:** the power or right to act, speak, or think as one wants without hindrance or restraint. **Choice:** an act of selecting or making a decision when faced with two or more possibilities. It all boils down to self-determination. That's it.

I remember working for a Fortune 500 company as a salesperson, and in my five-year tenure, I outlasted all five managers in our group – plus the director, head of sales, VP of sales, and the CEO. And yet, I was never the boss. A new person would come in and they would have the "magic bullet" plan to get everything on the right track, but it was really just the flavor of the month. They were justifying their own hiring and I had to go along for the ride. Let me give you some highlights. One of my favorites was dubbed, "10-4 out the door." Seriously. Managers went by all the desks to make sure you were gone. Yes, even when you had work to do in the office. Another was a "university program" to educate all the salespeople on current products, even though many had been there for years. Ironically, it started at 4:30 every afternoon in the office ... so much for "10-4 out the door." And a last gem was the collecting of business cards to verify you (me) were actually working. For all they knew, I could have just gone around asking for cards and not tried to make any sales. It was at that moment, with this last magic bullet, that I said, "thank you very much," and I was out.

Which brings us to you. You must have had "the moment," like the one I described, that brought you to this book. Maybe you didn't have the power to decide your own direction or priorities. Perhaps you didn't have the freedom to design your days. Or maybe you didn't have the power of choice in your daily work. An employee in past decades might be willing to stick out a situation like this because of what long-term employment and loyalty could bring them in retirement. However, I'm sure you have a general understanding that our world has changed and that long-term job security is now just a myth. Few successful pensions exist anymore, the middle class is shrinking and you've got big dreams that can't be fulfilled in your current gig.

Knowing what it was about the moment or moments that

moved you (or are moving you) to choose entrepreneurship can tell you a lot about yourself and a lot about how you want to design your own leadership experience. Take a moment to describe – in detail – those low points and those significant moments that have led you here:

_____

_____

_____

_____

_____

_____

_____

_____

_____

_____

_____

_____

_____

_____

_____

_____

_____

_____

_____

_____

_____

_____

Here are general themes I hear from people about the moments that pushed them to follow their dreams into entrepreneurship:

ONE

Like me, you are or were in corporate America and you know

your talent is not being utilized. Even worse, your most valuable asset – your time here on Earth – is being wasted. You have some savings and are willing to go into some debt to "run the show" because you know you can do it. You are great with people and money, but you know you don't have the knowledge and experience in this space to be a success … yet. You want to find a way in. The good news is … now you have.

TWO

You have never worked in corporate America and have always been a hustler (a much harder worker than most). You haven't had all the opportunities that others have had (family money or college, for example), but you make the most of them. You know there is a giant opportunity with cannabis and also know that if you had a system to follow that was trackable and repeatable, you could crush it. Keep reading, please.

THREE

You are already the owner of a successful small business. You keep hearing about cannabis but are not a user of the product, and so you're not sure if you fit in. Maybe you have done so well for yourself that you are, frankly, a little bored right now? Perhaps you see the opportunity here to not only make a lot of money but also get your juices flowing and feel excited about owning a business again. I don't use cannabis products either, and in this book, I'll tell you why that is the perfect position to be in.

FOUR

You are in your sweet spot. You are a serial entrepreneur and have successfully exited some companies with a ton of capital.

You, being a visionary, know there is something in the cannabis industry, but haven't found the right voice that syncs to your ear. Good for you; you're in the right spot too.

Between knowing the things that you no longer want as a part of your life and knowing how you are currently positioned, you should be able to enter the work associated with this book with more clarity. If none of the scenarios I just described really landed for you, please take a few minutes to write where you are today (being totally honest). Remember, this is for you. Don't cheat yourself. Why you are reading this book?

_____

_____

_____

_____

_____

_____

_____

_____

_____

_____

_____

_____

_____

_____

_____

_____

Let me give you the top ten reasons to become an entrepreneur (the specifics of power, freedom, and choice):

- It's an opportunity to change the world and solve problems – to make a real impact.

- You can have your say with everything – full autonomy.

- You make your own schedule and choose your daily work.

- No one controls you (you're "the man" or "the woman").

- You can dream as big as you want.

- The potential for income and growth is unlimited.

- There's an opportunity to get a huge financial gain from your hard work – more than you could at a 9-to-5 (no caps, no politics, and no ladder …).

- You can create more personal freedom away from work.

- You can make a positive difference in the lives of others.

- You can leave a legacy for your family that speaks to your unique accomplishments.

Honestly, it just feels fucking great to play your own game and win!

STRESSED OUT

A TRIBE CALLED QUEST

Entrepreneurship: Why Not.

WHENEVER I EVALUATE A CHOICE, I look at all sides carefully. I know that sounds obvious, but many people fail to explore all of the possibilities fully. There is a huge downside to entrepreneurship that I have to cover, and honestly, it's why this book will help you so much. We're going to look at the benefits and drawbacks of the business so you don't go in blind. The choice to be an entrepreneur should be a thoughtful business choice – not just a whim. Given the nature of entrepreneurship, you may also need to consider the personal elements of making this choice. If you have a family, they will be going through this same shift along with you. Everyone is along for the ride, financially and emotionally. Relationships can be intensely stressed by money and unbalanced amounts of time spent working. And if your relationship isn't ready to take that on, the stress of your relationship will, in turn, impact your success in the business. Entrepreneurship isn't whimsical.

Stress kills. According to the Mayo Clinic, stress symptoms affect your body and your behavior. It states, "Stress that is left unchecked can contribute to many health problems such as high blood pressure, heart disease, obesity, and diabetes."

Here is their list of classic stress symptoms:

ON YOUR BODY	ON YOUR MOOD	ON YOUR BEHAVIOR
• Headache • Muscle tension or pain • Chest pain • Fatigue • Change in sex drive • Stomach upset • Sleep problems	• Anxiety • Restlessness • Lack of motivation or focus • Feeling overwhelmed • Irritability or anger • Sadness or depression	• Overeating or undereating • Angry outbursts • Drug or alcohol misuse • Tobacco use • Social withdrawal • Exercising less often

You better believe that stress is going to deeply impact your personal and professional world, and being out on your own as an entrepreneur comes with guaranteed stress.

An article in *Entrepreneur.com* entitled, "7 Dark Truths of Entrepreneurship," lays out a list of the ugly side of entrepreneurship that can not only lead to the failure of a business endeavor but more critically can lead to intense personal stress (and perhaps personal failure). The seven truths they name are:

- You won't make money right away.

- Your personal life will suffer.

- Trying to juggle everything will take its toll on you.

- Your emotions will get the better of you.

- Nothing will happen the way you think it will.

- You'll make decisions that will haunt you.

- You are going to fail.

I doubt anyone who's tried to start and lead a business would argue with these seven dark truths. Why, then, do so many business books talk about strategy instead of stress? Why do so many people focus on the "how to" of their particular industry? Six of these seven items (all but the first) are about who you are, and yet so few leaders spend any time unpacking who they are, and how that shows up in their work. Entrepreneurship is tough and many fail. Sadly, the majority of entrepreneurs still focus on the actions, information, or methods instead of themselves as the engine of the whole operation. Why?

Maybe it's just me, but do you ever daydream that one day everything will be "right"? Like ... everything? No more problems with anything? For example, when you go public with your company and you have more money than you can spend, everything will be alright (hint: that will create a set of different problems). When you get your kids through college and they're on their way, everything will be alright (hint: you never stop worrying about them). Or when you become famous, you'll have no more worries? Bring on the personal chef, the personal trainer, piles of money, and tons of fans (hint: a whole bunch of bullshit is tied to being famous)! I believe most people shy away from doing the hard work of looking inward because they don't get that they *can't make it without mental health*. They're just blindly hoping that someday it will all simply work itself out.

Even Steve Jobs, arguably one of the most successful entrepreneurs of all time, who "made it" in all senses of the word, was never safe and free of problems.

There is disagreement about how Jobs left Apple – he says he was fired; others say he was forced out, and still others say he chose to leave. Either way, does it matter how or why he left Apple? He was out of the company he had created and it must have been humiliating for him. Can you imagine the little details that come with leaving a company you are tied to so emotionally? You get the pleasure of turning in your security cards, giving up your sweet parking spot, removing your personal things, and walking past offices in the building that, without you, would not be there at all. It would suck for anyone, but this happened to Steve fucking Jobs. Incredible. Nice work, John Sculley.

No one is safe, so if you want to be sure you can handle the personal strain and stress of entrepreneurship, you should take the first two sections of this book seriously. Scared? That's okay. I believe it's worth all the risk, but you have to prepare the right way, and that begins with living and leading as a strong, healthy person. Working on yourself also will help you have clear communication with your family and set them up to feel supported and to share in your vision. In entrepreneurship, like the military, everybody serves.

You're not going to win all the time. Kobe Bryant, largely considered one of the five greatest players in professional basketball history, only won five world championships in a multi-decade career. Only! But consider that he lost two NBA championships and thirteen different times the Lakers never made it to the Finals. That means for fifteen years of his twenty-year career, he and his team didn't complete the team's goals for the season. Yet he is largely known for his legendary drive and success.

If Kobe isn't enough inspiration, think about this simple idea:

PLANES ARE SAFEST ON THE GROUND, BUT THAT'S NOT WHAT PLANES ARE FOR.

PEOPLE

RAY CHARLES

People Make All the Difference

THE SONG *PEOPLE* COMES FROM ONE OF MY FAVORITE records when I was a kid, "Ray Charles Invites You To Listen." My dad listened to it a lot, which influenced my love for the album and ultimately, my love for high-quality music. As a father, I love to play great music for my boys. Their favorite sing-along is *Hit the Road Jack* (also by Ray). Whatever you think of your parents, their influence – positive and negative – undoubtedly lives through you. My boys never got to meet my dad, but I imagine someday they'll continue some of the music traditions we share with their own children. Three generations after my dad died (and possibly more), he will be impacting the rituals and bonding moments in my family. On the negative side, my dad smoked at least two packs of unfiltered Lucky Strikes every day. Back in those days, he smoked in the office, house, and car. Since I was the younger brother and smaller, I sat behind him in the car and noticed a yellow stain on his window from ashing his smokes, and from the endless contrail of smoke that billowed behind them. To this day, when I pass someone on the street who is smoking, it literally smells like home to me. We want to build on positive things about home (even if they carry a load of irony) and resist the negatives.

When the boys were singing the other day, it got me thinking about the influence of people in general. I thought, "Is there anything that I do in life, any decision I make, that isn't based on people?" The answer was no. Every decision – small and big – happens as a result of someone's influence, or my attempt to influence others. It was a powerful realization.

Think about it: is there anything more draining or consuming than being in a bad relationship? How about being immersed in a divorce or a custody battle? Going to an interview for a job? Have you had a terrible boss? Did you experience cliques when you were in school? Have you had surgery? Have you raised children? Ever engaged in social media? Led a team of people? Sat on a jury?

PEOPLE ARE THE X FACTOR OF LIFE.

As a budding (or developing) entrepreneur working as the head of your business, you may often feel like the star of the show – you're in the spotlight. It's critical that you remember everything you do is powered by the people around you. The most successful businesspeople figure out how to deeply understand, learn from, and influence the people around them. If you don't have an appreciation for the power of people, you probably won't succeed in entrepreneurship. This book is all about people (you and others), and this chapter is going to ground you in my "people philosophy." I'm going to take the mystery out of sales, leadership, culture, customer service, and management. Here it is:

THERE IS NOT ENOUGH BUSINESS IN RELATIONSHIPS AND NOT ENOUGH RELATIONSHIP IN BUSINESS.

It's a simple idea, but understanding and applying it can make all the difference in your success personally and professionally. Businesses and marriages both fail at an alarming rate. No one starts a business or gets married intending to fail, so what's going wrong?

Let's tackle the first half of the problem first – not enough business in relationships. When dating, how many times have you overlooked potential red flags, or even blatant red flags, because you were so excited about the fun: the sex, the new experiences, the excitement of it all? It seems unromantic to talk about the business side of a relationship (core values, finances, living styles, how each of you handles stress, how you want to raise kids, etc.). People skip it until the relationship is serious, until they've already made a commitment, and then uncover that their relationship is missing sound fundamentals.

In business, people make the reverse mistake. People discount critical human relationships and the opportunity to create deeper connections. They ignore the significance of sharing deeper personal values, and think they're doing that in the spirit of "staying focused on the work." The relationships and the people ARE the work, and the business owners who understand that make sure that relationships live in their work daily.

Let me tell you a quick story about the Beach Boys. As you may already know, the group was comprised of three brothers, a cousin and a fifth member who was a good friend. The Beach Boys rank 12th on Rolling Stone magazine's 100 Greatest Artists of All Time, so they were legit musicians – not one-hit wonders. Dennis Wilson, one of the brothers, and his cousin, Mike Love, could not have been fundamentally more opposed, though. Mike Love, as the frontman, thought of the band as a serious business, whereas Dennis Wilson thought it was a setting to pick up women. Mike was married and serious about his relationship, whereas Dennis might bring home Charlie Manson and the "Manson women" to have orgies at his house. Mike drank alcohol recreationally, whereas Dennis was an alcoholic. The situation escalated to the point where they couldn't even see each other before a show, each filed a restraining order against the other, and to add insult to injury, a 37-year-old Dennis impregnated Mike's daughter, who was 17 at the time. Dennis married her, but somehow I don't think that helped the situation.

Here's the point when it comes to investment in people:

If these two men who had so many similarities (cousins, men, same race, same profession…) could fall apart, then we know that similarities alone do not connect us. Similarities without any other effort give us very little. You can like, respect, work with, care about, be in relationships with, be inspired by, and love people who don't look like you. Right? They aren't the same color, aren't the same sex, aren't from the same countries, have different styles, like different music, and are all shapes and sizes – and still it all works out – as long as we commit to the fundamentals at the core of the relationship. It's the depth that matters in both relationships and business, not the surface.

VALUES ARE THE GLUE THAT BIND US

Here is a list of questions you can use for relationships (R), business (B), or both:

R: What are your relationship deal-breakers? (shows how much they know themselves)

B: What are your deal-breakers with a manager/employee relationship?

R: How do you define financial success? (shows if they have a clear vision/financial values)

B: How does this opportunity fit into your financial goals?

R: If taking a trip, do you plan everything or go with the flow? (reveals how do they approach life)

B: When taking on a task, do you plan it or go with the flow?

B/R: You can have dinner with anyone, living or dead, so who, why, and what do you ask? (reflects their values)

R: What are some issues you know you have? (shows if they are self-aware)

B: Honestly, what are some challenges you have had at other jobs?

R: Do you want children? (reveals if they have future plans and values that align with yours)

B: How do you balance personal time and work time?

R: How did your childhood affect your thoughts on raising children? (shows self-awareness)

B: What are some of the challenges you've overcome to get to this point in your career?

R: What will we do if we need to keep the spark going sexually? (reveals if they are willing to work)

B: Are you committed to being in communication and working on solutions before quitting?

R/B: What is your favorite movie and why? (reflects their values)

R: If you won $50 million in the lottery, what are the first ten things you would do? (shows their values)

B: If you won $50 million in the lottery, would we ever see you again?

Many, many small businesses fail, and almost 50 percent of marriages fail. The numbers are even worse for people in committed relationships but who are not married. That is an awful lot of failure for people who are actually trying to succeed.

If who we are matters more than what we know, then as entrepreneurs and significant others, we should be spending more time getting to know who someone is and how they could fit into our plans. You can teach a smart person anything they need to know, provided they are willing.

Here are some ways we will explore this concept in the book:

- How could a systematic approach to sales help you and your employees achieve better results?

- How do you structure emotionally charged conversations with people for success every time?

- How do relationships increase sales more than features/benefits?

- How do you elicit what people want to tell you as a boss/leader/friend but are afraid to?

- How does the consumption of cannabis connect to our 4,000-year-old connection to human gratification?

GET REAL

KNOW YOURSELF

THE REAL ME

THE WHO

The Value of Vulnerability

YOU ARE PREPARING TO EMBARK on an exciting journey, and the better you know yourself, the more prepared you will be to face whatever the journey presents. The first step in knowing yourself is being honest with yourself, and that requires vulnerability. The dictionary defines vulnerability as "the quality or state of being exposed to the possibility of being attacked or harmed, either physically or emotionally."

I came up with my own definition that I want you to consider alongside the official one: *Vulnerability is the key to human connection*. I believe human connection is the center of life, business and personal, and I want you to be excellent at it.

Think about it. Aren't there moments when you really know someone is being real with you and that changes something in you? There is a legitimate and true window into the heart and soul of another human being, and you can feel it when someone really opens that window. It sounds something like this:

It was my fault.

I'm sorry that I hurt you.

When I feel upset about something else, I take it out on you.

I got fired from my job today, and even though I'd like to blame them, it was my fault.

Sometimes I feel insecure with myself and ...

I've worked on this _____ and sometimes I fall short.

I worked really hard and I failed.

I'm the reason we haven't kept in touch. I really miss you and I'm sorry.

You are so special to me. I'm sorry I don't tell you every day.

I will do anything I can to make this right for you. What can I do?

Some of you reading this have wanted others to say these things to you for years. If they did, wouldn't you just hug them? Wouldn't those hurt feelings and disappointments and pains start to wash away, allowing you to get back to the loving connection you are longing for? People's vulnerability moves and inspires us. It is brave and strong to be vulnerable because it takes relationships deeper, and that is where the gold is.

There is a scene from The Sopranos series that exemplifies this point perfectly. John Sacrimoni, "Johnny Sack" is a mob guy who has a wonderful wife, Jinny, who struggles with her weight. Johnny loves her as she is, but she is always trying to lose weight "to be like the other wives." She starts going on diets and trying new things. One day Johnny is leaving to go out for the day and forgets his sweater, so he goes back to the house, and as he enters, he yells for his wife but he can't find her. He finally finds her in the basement huddled over a box of candy, cookies, and various junk foods, and he gets upset. They both start yelling at each other, attacking each other and defending themselves ... then this authentic moment happens:

Johnny: "Do you have any idea what you've done?"
Jinny: "What do you mean?"
Johnny: "You lied to me! You lied!"
Jinny: "I know I've gained weight over these last few years, I see the other wives ... the way men look at them ..."
Johnny: "Don't I look at you like that? [She nods] Haven't I always? [She nods] It was your idea, all this dieting nonsense."
Jinny: [weeping now] "I want you to be proud of me."
Johnny: "I am proud of you. I love you." [strong embrace]

That script flipped what could have been a huge fight with days-long resentment and sadness, but because she had the courage to be real and vulnerable, it turned out golden. That one moment – it opens up a space in another and creates empathy so they don't go for the jugular, but instead respond with warmth and love. From adversarial to deep human connection – in just one quick minute.

You've heard the saying, "Keeping up with the Joneses." It means comparing yourself to others – friends, neighbors, and associates – as a benchmark for how well you are doing financially. I have a saying that is called, "Not keeping up with the fake bullshit that is slowly killing our spirits and relationships." I'm kidding about the saying, of course, but the point is that we as people keep trying to hide and minimize our pain, failures, and shortcomings as if to appear perfect or have it all together. It is insane. Being flawed and having problems is what makes us human. It makes us vulnerable.

The best leaders know that exposing their own vulnerability establishes a safe environment for those around them. As you read this book, I hope you will see that I try to model that level of emotional exposure and work to parrot that message throughout.

In fact, I'll go first in exposing my own shortcomings:

I want you to know that this photo has NOT been touched up in any way. It really is as bad as it looks. The miracle of this image? That is a legitimate smile.

I had moved from Virginia to California the day before eighth grade started,

Todd in 8th Grade

and showed up at school, like that: crooked tie, braces, slacks, loafers, and a bowl haircut, when everyone else was wearing tank tops, shorts and flip-flops. Let's just say California was a bit of a culture shock after Virginia. That one move cost me a year of friends, too ... seriously. Appearance matters in the *Golden* state more than most places, and let's just say I was a little slow to the party.

In other self-flaw disclosures:

- I once trusted a friend and lost $50,000 in six weeks on an investment in China.

- I had five houses before the 2008–2009 recession, and lost over $2 million when four out of five were foreclosed upon (it took me five years of fighting with a major bank to keep the last one).

- I had $200,000 in the bank and wanted to invest in the Google IPO and I may never know why, but I never pulled the trigger.

- I sometimes get so frustrated with traffic that I literally can't believe we landed men on the moon and brought them back safely over fifty years ago, and we still can't properly manage vehicles on a roadway.

- I talk fairly fast, and when people, even my mom, can't understand me the first time, I get so impatient that I sometimes won't repeat what I had just said, simply because I'm irritated.

- I'm so stubborn that when I'm in the middle of a project, such as this book, and someone suggests another way that might work better, I initially won't give in.

- I like to win. For example, while playing Chutes and Ladders with my four-year-old son recently, I landed on the chute that sends you back to the bottom. Rather than acquiesce, I started thinking of a way to cheat, basically. I didn't, but for a split second I wanted to … it was an impulse.

I could go on … I'm not proud of these things. They are my shortcomings.

BRING THE PAIN

METHOD MAN

Identifying Your Pain and Its Symptoms

PART OF WHAT CONTRIBUTES TO OUR WEAKNESSES and our failures is the remnant pain in our lives. When we respond emotionally in any given situation, it means that we aren't in control because of that pain, which often causes poor results. Therefore, part of getting real before you move forward in becoming a cannabis entrepreneur involves spending time defining your pain and its symptoms so that you can anticipate issues and avoid pitfalls. Our pain limits us and we can only lift those limits by dealing with the core issues.

In America, and likely elsewhere too, we often deal with the symptoms of our pain, but usually not the root cause, and that is because the symptoms are so much easier to identify. There is a disease called Allodynia, and its symptom is that the light touching of your skin or brushing of your hair feels extremely painful. It's essentially a pain response to things that usually do not cause pain. The interesting thing is you can't tell from the outside if someone has it. Not dealing with the core of our pain is like that. Someone says something or does something that triggers the pain and hurt from the root cause. Our symptom is an overreaction to the stimulus. The other day, I was driving with my son, and he was playing around with a plastic sword. He pushed it into the side of my neck. It was harmless and no big deal. But my reaction was extreme for the situation. I turned quickly, knocked it off, and yelled, "Don't do that when I'm driving!" He looked shut down. I felt terrible. The truth is my Dad used to grab my brother and me by the back of the neck and kind of move us around when he was upset. My reaction to my son was like a flashback to my Dad's treatment, but it took place with my son. Wrong place, wrong person. I pulled over and apologized. I just told him it was my fault, not his. Showing your children that you can and will apologize will do wonders at setting the example. Working on yourself and identifying your "Allodynia-responses" is a continuous work in progress. In a little bit, you will have an opportunity to share some about yourself.

When your reactions seem disproportionate to someone else, it's in part because it isn't their problem you are in pain, and isn't their fault that the real problem hasn't been solved. The ball is in and always was in your possession to do the right thing. Doing the work of identifying the source of your true pain will allow you to avoid disproportionate responses to life's "light bumps" – the type that you should be able to work through quickly and without drama.

Since I obviously can't have a one-to-one conversation with you directly, what I want you to do is answer a question, but I need you to be honest. What is going on with you? If you have hard life issues you are dealing with, then be as verbose as possible with your answer. Be vulnerable. If nothing is dragging you down, then that is an excellent place to be, and you should feel extremely proud. Either that or you need to dig a little bit deeper. Everyone has something ...

... addiction perhaps?

I know you don't want to hear this, but in my opinion, there is no logical reason for human beings to be addicted to anything, be it pain pills, alcohol, cigarettes, sex, their jobs, or starving themselves. All of these addictions stem from our attempts to treat or respond to the symptoms of our pain, but the sad truth is that people are dying as we ignore the overall cause. In 2016, for the first time ever, more people in the US died of prescription pain pill overdoses than were killed in homicides.

THERE IS NO EXTERNAL SOLUTION FOR AN INTERNAL PROBLEM.

We, as human beings, try to avoid pain as much as possible. So much so that we will engage in "crazy" activities to mask it, hide it, and bury it. The problem is that this pain is killing us.

I'm going to talk about pain directly. In fact, you and I are going to talk about it right now. So get ready to be uncomfortable again. Many of you are likely reading this book because you are looking for a way to change your life, your circumstances, and your legacy. Dealing with the pain that has likely held you back represents a big, first step in the right direction, so power through!

What are typical emotional responses (symptoms) caused by pain? Are you dealing with any of the following?

- Are you edgy?
- Does the voice in your head (the one that's talking to you right now) talk down to you?
- Do you feel like you'll never get it right?
- Do you feel like it's too late?
- Do you feel like you'll never get out of debt?
- Do you feel like you let your family down?
- Do you dismiss heartfelt compliments from others?
- Do you daydream about winning the lottery?
- Do you make excuses for why things won't work out, so you don't have to take a real risk?
- Do you avoid trying so that you avoid failing?

Now let's get to the nasty (real), less-palatable symptoms:

- Are you quick to anger?
- Do you yell at your children?
- Do you have road rage?
- Do you lie to people?
- Do you cheat?
- Do you secretly criticize people who (you think) are doing better than you?
- Do you find ways to escape your real life, like reading, watching TV, and watching sports?
- Do you abuse alcohol, drugs, and/or tobacco?
- Do you use porn to control or avoid intimacy?
- Do you abuse pain medication?
- Have you contemplated suicide?

I have done some of these things. Why? I have been in pain at different times in my life – some of which I named earlier. We all have a version of this list if we're being honest with ourselves. It is what makes us human. I feel if we can connect fully with the nastiest feelings we have, or things we do, we can get real with how the pain of being unfulfilled is hurting us, and we can find the motivation to take action.

Also, in America we have more people in our prisons and the highest level of drug abuse than any other country. We suffer from a pain that comes from our personal histories, but there's another side of it too –the pain that results from being unfulfilled. Perhaps you want to pay for your children's education and know you can't. Maybe you know you have no retirement funds, or like many people, your funds are woefully short. Whatever the cause, when you know you haven't lived up to your potential and when you have the desire to succeed but don't know how to make it happen, you lose hope.

Hope is essentially when you want something to happen or have a desire for something to happen. Hope without a plan, strategy, or system, however, converts to a wish. Wishes are more distant than our original hopes: they are the things we want but don't really think are going to happen. When fundamental dreams become distant wishes, you are experiencing hopelessness. Hopelessness leaves people feeling despondent, depressed, and pessimistic, and at that point, most people passively abandon their fate – their potential. Unfortunately, this pain isn't always dramatic. If it was, we might do more to reverse it. Often though, it's a low-grade feeling of disappointment every time you're reminded you can't have or do something you want.

For example, imagine you need to buy a car. You know that a vehicle is not an asset but rather a liability because it decreases in value the moment you drive it off the lot. You also know financing a car is a bad long-term move because you end up paying more than the car is worth. However, to save up for a new, safer, more modern car could take years. You don't really want to wait that long, so you finance the car and never own it until it is paid off. When you drive it, you often feel good about its safety and reliability. That's great, but sometimes you're reminded of how the financing has set you back, left you unable to put away the kind of money each month that you would like to save for your children's education, your retirement, and your dreams. You're reminded daily that you haven't made it to that successful and secure place where you could walk in and buy a car outright. That's low-grade pain.

When any pain is affecting your life, it robs you of happiness, freedom, satisfaction, relationships, love, connectivity, and peace of mind.

You ARE capable of getting to that cash-rich place, however, and we are going to help you break the cycle of disappointment. We are going to help you turn your hope into action that lets you turn your dreams into reality.

To do that, you have to begin by being brutally honest about what is really going on with you: what pain you are in, how you deal with it, what hopes you had that you may have lost belief in and what you have left on the table.

Then, you need to do the complete opposite of what most people do and what you may be doing right now – avoiding, procrastinating, hiding, pretending, faking, and self-medicating – to fully experience the pain you are in. When you sit in that place and fully experience it, the only clear path is the one out of it. This is the point you want to get to in order to make a change. If you're holding on to any of it, then it's going to hold you back. When you're clear about it and have the courage to face it down, you can then make a declaration of a new future and find a new path to get where you want to go.

I recommend you take a few hours and get totally real about your life – pain, hopelessness, and happiness; what's working and what's not working – and find a new level of connectedness to yourself (you'll likely need more space than is provided here, but if you start here you'll always have a record of this reflection to guide how you will move forward). This is between you and yourself, so don't hold back ...

My pain symptoms:

_____

_____

_____

_____

_____

_____

_____

_____

_____

_____

_____

_____

_____

_____

_____

_____

_____

_____

_____

Possible sources of my pain (personal: relationships, parents, family, school, lack of fulfillment, unmet potential, etc.):

_____

_____

_____

_____

_____

_____

_____

_____

_____

_____

_____

_____

_____

Possible sources of professional pain (failure, fired, bad investments, unmet potential, etc.):

_____

_____

_____

_____

_____

_____

_____

_____

_____

_____

_____

_____

_____

_____

_____

You may be asking—*"Okay Todd, thank you for that. Now that I got all raw and dredged up all that shit, what the hell am I supposed to do?"*

Well, the first part of moving past the pain is to recognize it. The second, and most important, part is to feel the pain. Sit with it. Or as OutKast would say, "Marinate on that." Why? Because when you stop faking, lying, masking, covering up and pretending it's not really there, then you get fully present to how badly you feel about certain things. Then and only then will you start to realize what it has cost you. And when you really start to add up that cost, the ONLY CHOICE is to start taking the actions necessary to solve it. Don't worry, you already know what actions to take. In fact, knowing what you should be doing, and feeling guilty about not doing it, is actually another symptom of people not moving honestly through their pain. Surface these feelings and experience them instead of masking them. At the end of the book you will create a personal declaration to drive you forward and explicitly name the action you need to take.

I WISH

STEVIE WONDER

Drive Your Legacy

VERY LIKELY, YOUR REFLECTIONS ON PAIN will connect you back to experiences you've had in your life. Experiences are underrated. Period. Giving experiences the importance they deserve is not about living in the past, but rather an acknowledgment that you have learned from them in a positive way that moves you forward. One reason people underrate their experiences, big and small, is that many people live as if they are not going to die – and not in the "seize the day" way you might hope. Instead, most people simply undervalue their time, because while they intellectually know they're going to die, they don't really appreciate their time as if they might die today, tomorrow, next year or in the next five years. If people lived like they were going to die – not recklessly but aware of the value of their time – they would take a lot more away from their experiences because they would value them more.

How many times have you half-assed a thank you, a good-bye, or an "I love you"? Or worse, how long have we let small experiences fester and become bigger, and then not forgiven someone we love just because we believed we were right? Too many times! I share a very personal story at the end of the book about my Dad and our relationship challenges, and ultimately our victory. If human beings don't invest in allowing our experiences to consciously move us forward – reaching higher or having a better connection with someone – we're wasting our experiences.

Now, go back to your reflections on your pain and its symptoms, and add anything else that has come to mind, small or big, that you have experienced and that you need to acknowledge. Add anything that could offer you wisdom as you make a change and move forward. For all the good and all the bad, take the necessary time to make sure you are valuing the time you've already had in this world. That makes the time you have left seem even more precious. This time, go beyond your pain to write down things you've learned and things you value. Also, think about regrets. I believe if you don't have regrets, you aren't paying attention. Again, these lines may not be enough space for deep reflection, just a record of how you started it ...

_____

_____

_____

_____

_____

_____

So how will you be your best self and live fully conscious of your path through life? I want to be sure you see how doing the work we've just done, every day of your life, is critical to leaving the legacy you want to leave in this world.

If you have your own children or are around children often, you know they are the best humans in so many ways. Aren't they? There is a freedom, an authenticity, and a genuine silliness about them. We can learn a lot by letting the way kids interact with the world remind us of how to see the best in people, ourselves, and the planet. Stevie Wonder's song, the title song of this chapter, is about wishing, as adults, that we could get back to that freedom we had as children. As adults, we get burdened with the heavy things in life. I'm not suggesting we take important things lightly, but can't we make sure we don't let the seriousness of those important things change how we respond to everything?

The opposite of being free and living presently is death. My death waits for me as yours waits for you. As I mentioned, most people don't value their life with death in mind. This unfortunate perspective not only means we take much less from our experiences, but it also means we are not constantly shaping our time so that we would be proud of it if we suddenly ran out of time. We are not taking advantage of the opportunity to leave a legacy in all that we do. Instead, we humans spend a ridiculous amount of time trying to extend our lives.

I saw a book in a store the other day, and the book was titled, *How To Not Die*, and I thought to myself, *Whoever wrote this is a baby. Grow up, man*! Rod Serling was the genius behind *The Twilight Zone,* and while he didn't write the following quote, it is a doozy from an episode of Twilight Zone (a lot of wisdom in that show) that always speaks to me:

"It's death that gives this world its point. We love a rose because we know it will eventually be gone. Whoever loved a stone?"

A crucial part of getting real is accepting that you will eventually be gone, knowing what you want your legacy to be, and then being sure you value that legacy so it drives what you do every day.

Keeping in mind all that you've reflected on in this section, I want you to write down what you want your legacy to be. Think of it this way: if you knew you were going to die in one year, what would you still want to complete? What would you want to be true for your family? How about your community? What set of experiences will create the legacy you want to leave. What do you want people to say about you when you are gone? (This frame immediately makes you cut out a lot of bullshit, doesn't it?)

_____

_____

_____

_____

_____

_____

_____

_____

_____

_____

_____

_____

_____

_____

_____

_____

_____

_____

_____

_____

_____

Tom Stewart, a man I liked a lot and had tremendous respect for, died suddenly on Valentine's Day. He was not a good friend only because he was older than me and a certified billionaire, which would actually put him "out of my league," so to speak. Just how rare is it to be a billionaire in America? There are 540 out of 323 million people. So if 1 percent of the US population equals 3.23 million, then just 0.00016 percent of the US population falls into the billionaire class.

Tom was a great family man. He was generous, too. Whenever he hosted a dinner party, as a gift, he always put a copy of the latest book he was reading on your plate, plus a few stories about why it was important. The last one he gave me was *Genghis Khan*, which should give you a hint of his organizational powers. He was a true original. An adventurer. His completion of the Pacific Crest Trail from Mexico to Canada, with his family and on horseback, was the stuff of legends. So was his Jeep Safari across the entire continent of Africa.

The day he died, he and his wife, their five-year-old daughter, the family dog, and a pilot were flying their helicopter from their ranch in Flagstaff to Phoenix when they crashed and everyone on board died. The NTSB theory was that his daughter was sitting on his lap and may have pushed down the helicopter controls. Either Tom or the pilot pulled them back up quickly, and that bent the rotor blades to the point that they struck the tail and came apart. The manufacturer had recently repaired one of the blades, and witnesses said pieces were falling off the doomed copter before it came down. In the end, does it really matter what actually happened? No, they are gone.

I think of these people often and the great loss it is to everyone who knew them. I also think, perhaps morbidly, about the fact that this guy was a winner and had won so many times, and what was he thinking while this was happening?

"It can't end like this, can it?"

"We'll make it somehow."

"I've got to protect my daughter!"

"Maybe I won't make it, but she has to!"

A man who seemed to have destiny on his side so often didn't have it that day. In the realm of you-can't-make-this-shit-up, this man, his family, and his business had been headquartered in Washington state. He had relocated everything to Arizona prior to the accident because of new stringent inheritance taxes that were levied in the Seattle area. Even though he lost his life, his surviving family ended up with more, because of that move. Even in death, he won a victory for his family.

Folks, do me a favor and remember this story because believe me, the last thing Tom was thinking when he woke that day was that he was going to die. Be ready.

How can you and I be prepared to die each day, if not satisfied, at least at peace with it? The only way to be prepared to die every day is to live your life to its fullest and get the most from each experience you have. People who know me well, really well, are careful what topics they bring up with me because they know I'm all-in on everything.

The joke around me is, "Don't let Todd find out about something you like because he'll start finding ways to deliver it to you … all the time!"

The reality is that these acts are far from a joke. Let me give you a few examples. Like most kids, my son was a huge fan of the movie series *Cars*. You may know that the film's star car is named Lightning McQueen. You may not know that there are probably fifteen versions of McQueen toys: Dinoco McQueen, Cactus McQueen, Ice Racer McQueen, Tumbleweed McQueen, Dirt Track McQueen, Fabulous Lightning McQueen, and there is even a Primer Grey McQueen, for when he is emotionally depressed in the movie. Seriously, my son has all of the McQueen action figures (cars) and then some. My younger son is obsessed with trash trucks. Not only does he have toy versions to play with and books about them, but when he sees one, it's, "Tash tuck! Tash tuck!" The first time he screamed it, I mean at the top of his lungs, I almost pulled over. I didn't know what the hell was happening. Now, when we spot one (and sometimes it's quite possible we just might go looking) we follow them in the alleys and streets, as time allows. I will park my truck and run up to them and say, "Hey, I'm sorry, I know this seems weird but I'm not stalking you or spying for the city, my son just wants to watch you pick up trash cans for as long as we can." These folks work hard and are always very pleasant. I literally know the routes and which days are for what: trash or recycling or compost.

Someone else who once shared with me their love for salt one day received some rare, large-kernel salt from Mexico, and then later some Himalayan salt and finally a book about the history of salt. After I'm dead, no one I've formed a relationship with is going to say I didn't give it my all or that I could have done more to foster friendship. Plus, the whole concept of "It is better to give than to receive" is so true.

If I see an opportunity to impact someone's life in a positive way or to constructively point out something that is missing – in the spirit of them having a better quality of life – I will do or say just about anything to make that happen. Sometimes it comes across like I'm stepping over the line. If so, I just clean it up. How? I apologize, tell them I love them and sincerely ask them to forgive me. This is the main thread of my life. I start with this at the beginning of this book in hopes that this book has a positive impact and allows you to live your life more fully.

Both in your personal declaration and in the work you will do to create your mission statement and choose values for your business, this reflection should be at the foundation. People who work for you and customers who buy from you will be moved by your ability to speak deeply and meaningfully about your understanding of yourself and your life. Remember, if you choose to open or retain a cannabis operation and/or dispensary, many of your customers will be coming to you looking for relief from pain during hard times in their lives. They will love the idea that the business they trust is run by a person in touch with vulnerability and humanity.

SOUND AND VISION

DAVID BOWIE

The Power of Affirmation and Vision

NOW THAT YOU HAVE SPENT TIME UNPACKING your pain and experiences so that you can embark on the next phase of your life with the necessary self-awareness, we need to take a moment to ensure you have the tools to keep living at the right level of awareness as you move forward.

You are probably aware that everything you read, see, hear, and experience is run through that little voice inside your head. You know, like the old cartoons with the angel on one shoulder and the devil on the other. You might be saying, "I don't have a voice in my head, Todd. That's crazy." Um, it's actually the one that just said that. Something that makes us uniquely human and natural survivors is that voice. It helps us evaluate and judge situations and decisions all the time. Do you have any idea how powerful the voice in your head is? It can literally be your greatest asset and your greatest enemy, if you let it. Your subconscious mind doesn't know what is real and isn't real, so if you tell yourself that you're the greatest, your mind will believe it. And if you tell yourself that you're the worst, your mind will respond to that too. Luckily, that voice in your head, which often functions mostly subconsciously, *can function consciously*. We can actually use the voice in our head – through things like affirmations and by envisioning what we want – to positively impact our outcomes.

Sound too "out there" for you? Well, consider this: *Psychology Today* reported, and studies have suggested, that mental practice can be almost as effective as physical training. One study, published in the *Journal of Sport & Exercise Psychology* in 1996, found that imagining weightlifting caused actual changes in muscle activity. Get your mind around that for a minute.

"Mental imagery impacts many cognitive processes in the brain: motor control, attention, perception, planning, and memory," researcher Angie LeVan wrote in *Psychology Today*. "So the brain is getting trained for actual performance during visualization. It's been found that mental practices can enhance motivation, increase confidence and self-efficacy, improve motor performance, prime your brain for success, and increase states of flow."

But visualizing is more than just thinking about an upcoming event. When athletes use visualization, they truly feel the event taking place in their mind's eye.

"During visualization, [the athlete] incorporates all of her senses into the experience," sports psychologist Dr. JoAnn

Dahlkoetter wrote in a blog post for *The Huffington Post* about a speed skater she works with. "She feels her forefoot pushing off the track, she hears her skating splits, and she sees herself surging ahead of the competition. She experiences all of the elements of her race in explicit detail before executing her performance."

In other words, top-tier athletes use the voices in their heads to create a sense of self that makes their performances even better in actuality.

Every day of your life is your performance, and entrepreneurship is your Olympics. You need to constantly train to be your best – learning to control that voice inside your head so that what you see and hear aligns perfectly with what you want. What you tell yourself about yourself and the world you live in – literally changes your world. Your viewpoint of the world actually *creates* your world.

You know there are people who think the Moon landing was the greatest accomplishment of mankind, and then there are people who think it was faked. Perhaps John Milton said it best, "The mind is its own place and, in itself, can make a heaven out of hell or a hell out of heaven." So, start practicing while you read this book. Any time a negative thought pops into your head while reading (possibly stemming from your personal pain and self-doubt), make the conscious move to flip the message. How?

For example:

THE UNCONSCIOUS MESSAGE	THE FLIPPED CONSCIOUS MESSAGE
This seems too complicated.	I'm excited to learn how to do this well and I'm glad I found a resource that has the details I need.
This seems too risky.	This is going to add some excitement into my life.
It seems like this industry changes all the time.	I'm never going to get bored doing this work.
I might put a ton of work in and still fail.	If I do all this work, I will have learned a ton. I am going to succeed.
I don't have the money to get started.	I am going to figure out how to finance this.
I don't have the time to do this.	I waste a lot of my time already, and now I'm going to fill that time more meaningfully. -or- If I engage my community in this dream, I can schedule the time.
Todd did this, but I don't think I'm like him.	I have unique skills and experiences that I can use to help me succeed.
I'm starting too late to take advantage of this opportunity.	I'm going to dive into this now because there's no time to waste.

It sounds cheesy, but it is actual science. When you harness the power of your brain, opportunities and successes will open up all around you and continue to open up as you move forward. It is like when you buy a new car and then suddenly see that model everywhere; they were always around you, but you shifted your awareness to notice them.

Take a moment and write down three doubts you have about going into the cannabis industry, and then flip the messages. If you can't flip the messages yet, I believe that by the time you finish this book, you will be able to go back to these doubts and write the flipped messages with confidence.

My Doubts:

_____

_____

_____

_____

_____

_____

_____

_____

Flipped Messages in My Control:

_____

_____

_____

_____

_____

_____

_____

_____

GET CLEAR

DEFINE YOUR VISION

TALK ABOUT THE PASSION

R.E.M.

Get Clear on Your Desired Impact – Your Why

I'M PASSIONATE ABOUT THE RESULT OF EVERYTHING I'm involved with, or I'm simply not doing it. Isn't it true that when you boil it down, most of us are really passionate about the difference we make, but not always the actual job we're doing? When I worked in telecommunications or at the gas station when I was fifteen or when I drove that tow truck in college, I can't say that my heart was full of passion, or that I was completely fulfilled. But through all those experiences, I learned more about what truly fills my heart and fulfills me – and for most other people too – and that is having a positive impact on others.

When I towed a car, for example, and there was a woman alone with the vehicle, I often thought to myself that she could be my mom sitting there, feeling uncomfortable on the side of the road, thinking about how much it was going to cost to fix and worrying about how to get around until it was fixed. In those moments, I felt like the "good guy" for someone who needed me. I was professional, quick, efficient, and kind. I showed up and took the pressure off and made things better. It was technically the job of moving a car from one place to another, but it was also making a small difference in that person's life during a difficult moment for them.

I have spent a lot of time thus far clarifying for you the impact I'm passionate about having, both personally and professionally, and I've aligned my professional pursuits so that I can have that impact. Clarity on this impact has become my WHY, the thing that underpins all of my pursuits. It's time for you to do the same. In the last chapter, you started to unpack your thinking about the pathway that will fulfill you in this industry. Now, we need to go deeper into defining the impact you want to have, *your why*, as it aligns with the legacy you already named in the first section of this book.

I'm specifically passionate about my family, friends, and many others "in the club" (my mantra is *take care of your people*), and my desired impact includes: leaving a positive example and providing financial security for my family; making a positive impression and a difference with people I might not know, while serving as an inspiration to others; and of course, being a leader.

What are you passionate about? (Be as detailed as possible and focus on impact.)

_____

_____

_____

_____

_____

_____

_____

_____

_____

_____

_____

_____

I had "the moment" while I was working in the grow room. I was gently scraping the tops of the soil in the pots to make sure the water flows evenly to all the roots (the tops can get crusty and limit water flow), and realized how I had mastered this process. It occurred to me that I bet there are a lot of people who would like to start out growing correctly with a system and have a follow-up system to support them. From there, I realized I am uniquely qualified with both the growing experience and the people experience to really motivate and lead people to change their future and legacy through this opportunity in cannabis. While I loved growing and working in a dispensary setting, I knew I belonged more in the business of helping, coaching, and serving others so they, too, can find success and navigate the myriad challenges.

Another warning, and this is corny but true: The greatest compliment I can receive from this book, my seminars, or services, is you coming up to me and saying, "Todd, thank you. This book was a stepping-stone in my path to the life and legacy I always wanted."

I'll warn you now: I may tear up, get emotional, and hug you right there because that is what it's all about for me. I want you to see this book as a tool, or a vehicle to help you get where you want to go and ultimately have the impact you want to have with your life, and/or with the money you make from this work.

I AM PASSIONATE ABOUT PEOPLE. I AM NOT PASSIONATE ABOUT MARIJUANA.

I always hear people talk about how passion and business must be intertwined: "follow your passion," or "if you follow your passion you'll never work a day in your life," or that, "if you are not passionate about your product, your brand can't be successful." Those are myths for a number of reasons:

First, sometimes you can be so passionate about something that it skews your objectivity. I bet many of you have been in relationships longer than you should have been or relationships you knew weren't good for you. How did that happen? Well, likely there was an element that hit on all cylinders and made you feel passionately toward each other: major physical attraction, great sex, or the exact same niche hobby. However, that passion blinded you to the less exciting, but critical components of the partnership that made you two unsuitable. Usually, our friends see the truth in these relationships before we do. This concept can also be true in business. Countless people have been truly passionate about what they produced, but ended up bankrupt.

Michael Gerber wrote a great book years ago called *The E-Myth*, in which the "E" stands for the entrepreneur. It was a revolutionary book because it recognized that the systematic approach to business is one of the only approaches that works. One example in the book discussed a woman who made pies. She originally just baked for her family and friends, but everyone told her that her pies were the greatest, and since she loved making them, they suggested that she should open a store and sell them. Everyone said she could make millions!

As the story goes, once she opened the store, she realized that making pies and dealing with customers – two things she knew she would love – were just minor parts of the overall business. She needed to deal with marketing, accounting, business legalities, real estate, inventory, vendors, financing, and more. She found that by the time she was done dealing with all those other things, she had limited time left to bake pies and engage with her customers. Her business was on a fast track to failure. That is, until she learned how to run it like an entrepreneur *AND* manager, and to hire people to do most of the administrative work.

This entrepreneurial phenomenon happens so often that several TV shows (*Restaurant: Impossible* and *Bar Rescue*) have capitalized on the notion of helping passionate people get their business systems together so they can actually make money. The pie-maker was hardly alone in her struggles.

Naming the *impact* you are passionate about and aligning your work to achieve that impact is the goal here. Almost everyone in business admires Warren Buffett. One of the biggest businesses he owns is Geico insurance. I have a strong suspicion that Warren Buffett doesn't wake up in the morning and feel giddy and passionate about owning an insurance company. I think he gets up and realizes that Geico insurance fits into his plan and his system for investing. Geico provides a good service to its customers, helps people, and makes an awful lot of money (in addition to the occasionally funny commercial). Buffett, I would guess, is passionate about finding and investing in excellent businesses, and making money that allows him to impact the world for good. Nothing is wrong with wanting to make money, as long as you identify the impact you want to create with that money. That will give you the right motivation for the work you will do to earn it. For example, your motivation might be to leave a legacy for your family, buy a house on the beach, or support causes you believe in.

The good news for you is that I have done a lot of the dirty work to create this book so that you will have focused passion, clear motivation, AND excellent systems. I encourage you to also engage with our website: Weedonomics101.com and the Weedonomics grower services because it has been proven repeatedly that few people succeed by just reading a book or attending a seminar. Motivation and change are difficult to maintain. I'll say it another way: motivation and change are fleeting. Why? Because motivation is temporary and change can be hard. Think about how many times you (or people you know) set up New Year's resolutions, only to quickly fall back into old ways. What you need is your why, plus systems, a plan and a coach – the guides that push and re-inspire you on the path to success.

In the NFL in 2014, fifteen teams had at least twenty-one coaches each, and four teams had twenty-four coaches each. Think about that for a second. There are only eleven players on the field at any one time and only fifty-three players on NFL final rosters. Now I know this is simple math, but that means you have at least two coaches for every player on the field at any given time. The point is, the greatest sports organizations in the world would not employ so many coaches if there was no actual benefit. The benefit is that a coach can see things about your game – while you're playing it – and give you feedback so that you can play at your best. Seventy percent of Fortune 500 CEOs have a coach of some sort. The New England Patriots, the most successful NFL team of the last twenty years, have a character coach whose sole job is to serve anybody and everybody in the organization with whatever they need help with. This book will coach you as you reflect, learn, and plan your path in the cannabis industry. I am inviting you to allow me to support you on that path. Your *why to* and my *how to*. Are you in?

Let's start unpacking how to align your personal passion with your business interests and professional strengths.

FOR THE LOVE OF MONEY

THE O'JAYS

Leveraging Your Impact

THERE IS NO QUESTION THAT THE RESULT of success in the marijuana industry includes making money. Money is a tool and when you have more of it, you can do more. We've talked about death, pain, experience, legacy, and impact, so let's just take a moment and talk about money, too (we can get into politics, religion, and sex another time in another book).

So many conversations happen about money. Who has it? How much do they have? How did they get it? Did they really earn it? How should you spend it? How shouldn't you spend it? How should you save it or invest it? Add to that all the judgment, jealousy, and sometimes respect and admiration that go along with having it. Here is the thing that you probably know, but you may not have had a chance to experience directly: No matter how you feel about it and regardless of what you do with it, everything is better when you have money. Period.

Food, clothes, wine, shoes, alcohol, cars, service, travel, houses, furniture, connections, education, experiences – it's all just better. I once dated a woman from a wealthy family. I don't know exactly how wealthy, because when you have that much, you don't have to talk about it. But there was enough for a private jet, limos everywhere, country clubs, mansions, ownership of professional sports teams, courtside season tickets to NBA games, the Super Bowl, the US Open, and the World Series. There was a condo by Central Park, a castle on the ocean in Pebble Beach, and so on. Once we flew the plane to San Francisco to see a concert (third row, center). I sat in the jump seat on takeoff and landing, which was amazing. When we landed, the limo pulled up to the plane to take us to the restaurant for lunch and then dropped us in front of the theatre for the show. Then it took us to dinner afterward and directly back to the plane and back home again. There was nothing like it, experience-wise. I don't think anyone should be ashamed of wanting or having money, but you have to be sure the decisions you make with it support what you truly want (your desired impact), or you can get lost in it.

I also want to be sure you remember that money is the icing on the cake. If the cake itself (your foundation) is not cooked properly, no amount of icing can cover up the cook's mistake. Similarly, money won't make a difference in the level of your happiness. Money just reveals more of who you already are and the personal problems you already had (see almost every lottery winner).

As you contemplate how you want to use the money you are

going to make in order to support your impact, here are a few examples of rich people who figured out incredible ways to do it.

Andrew Carnegie (from Carnegie Hall and Carnegie Mellon University) started creating his impact due to a dispute with a subscription library. To most of us, a public library has always been available and free. That was not the case in the mid-to-late 1800s. Books were exclusive and very expensive. The only way a common person had access to books was by paying for a membership. At seventeen, Carnegie couldn't afford the subscription, but being a very smart man, he wrote a letter to the main newspaper to state his case, and the library was opened to working men with no fee. Carnegie later went on to become the richest man in the world and maybe the richest American of all time, with a net worth of $480 million in 1901 ($312 billion in today's dollars). In his view, life was a three-step process: education, production, and philanthropy. He created the Carnegie library system, which built 2,509 libraries from 1883–1929, to give access to books to Americans across the country and the world.

Since you likely already know a lot about Bill Gates and Warren Buffett, two of the top richest Americans year after year, you know they follow in Carnegie's footsteps with their attention to using money for greater impact and philanthropy.

Did you know, however, that the Bill and Melinda Gates Foundation has $38 billion in assets? The primary aims of the foundation are to enhance healthcare and reduce extreme poverty on a global scale, and in America to expand educational opportunities and access to information technology. What I love about Buffett is that instead of saying, "Hey, I have to have my own foundation with my name on it," he understands that Gates has already built a great foundation, and so he simply gives to the

Gates Foundation so that his money can go even further. As of the writing of this book, he has donated $31 billion of his own money, and his company, Berkshire Hathaway, adds another $2 billion to the fund each year. That's an organization with serious resources!

Here are a few highlights of what the Gates Foundation has accomplished thus far:

- 12 million people have been tested and treated for tuberculosis.

- 500 million children have been vaccinated and seven MILLION lives have been saved.

- 7.3 million people with HIV have received treatment.

- There has been a 99 percent drop in polio worldwide and only one hundred cases worldwide have been reported since 2015.

- Children in Kentucky jumped from 34 to 64 percent career-ready when they graduated from high school.

- Homelessness has been reduced for families in the state of Washington by 35 percent.

- And so much more ...

If you're telling yourself that it is easy to make this kind of difference when you already have billions of dollars, you are right. However, monumental impacts can be made by making a declaration, sticking to it, and getting others involved in your vision. Consider the story of Amos Muzyad Yakhoob Kairouz – who later changed his name to Danny Thomas. Danny was a relatively unknown singer and actor who you might have described at the time as the classic "starving actor." During this tough time, Danny made a vow: if he found success, he would open a shrine dedicated to St. Jude Thaddeus, the patron saint of hopeless causes. Thomas never forgot his promise to St. Jude, and after becoming successful in the 1950s, he and his wife began traveling the United States raising additional funds to support his dream. With his own money and his work to help others invest in his vision, Danny created St. Jude's Children's Research Hospital in 1962.

Since its inception, St. Jude has treated children from all 50 states and around the world. Although it costs around $2.4 million *daily* to run the hospital, no families that have children being treated ever receive a bill. The hospital is a nonprofit organization. Danny followed through on his declaration to come to the service of "hopeless causes," and he has provided the opportunity to get not only treatment for illnesses feared untreatable, but also to do so without the incredible stress of a financial burden. Danny made a declaration at his lowest point and used it to fuel his drive to success.

As we already discussed in this book, what you tell yourself helps to define your reality. Imagine that you are successful in the cannabis industry. Write down what your net worth will be:

$_____

Now take a moment to brainstorm how you will use that money to satisfy your impact (think about what you want and what you will do).

EVERYBODY IS A STAR

SLY AND THE FAMILY STONE

Choosing Your Path

NOW WE'RE GOING TO GO DEEPER into two questions that are essential to Get Clear:

- What are my personal strengths?

- What are my professional strengths and weaknesses?

Answers to these questions will give you more insight into where you may be best suited to work in this industry.

Have you ever wondered how two or more people from the exact same parents, raised in the same house and under the same conditions, can in certain ways end up so very different? I love my brother and we get along great, but sometimes we wonder if we would be such good friends if we weren't brothers. The answer is probably no, and not in a negative way. I mean, I'm a dog person and he's a cat person. Enough said, right? We just see the world differently.

Some years ago, we took a driving trip through Baja, Mexico, and he bought a guidebook and maps and wanted a detailed plan of where we were going. I said something like, "Dude, let's get some cash and water at the border, and just go for it. We'll figure it out along the way."

He ended up getting sick and we stayed at a motel on the beach for three days doing nothing but reading books and talking until they shut off the electricity at 9:00 p.m. This downtime was not in the plan, but it ended up being fun. Without his preparation, we wouldn't have known where to go when he got sick, and without my ability to go with the flow, we wouldn't have turned the situation into the best it could have been. The point is we are a good balancing act, because at the end of the day, everyone has something great to offer. The reality is that you need all kinds of people to make a business successful. Knowing what you are good at, plus what skills you need to import, will help you define what part of the business most needs you.

Since the cannabis industry is specialized, we now have created entire industries to support it, including plumbers, electricians, HVAC (heating and ventilation and air conditioning), security, construction, cleaning crews, managers, customer service agencies, real estate, accounting, grow masters, and retail owners, plus myriad consultants in all these fields.

You don't need to grow or own a dispensary to participate in this space, although this book will give you a sturdy foundation for understanding both areas. That understanding will give all other business ideas or concepts an access point. If you have an understanding of how marijuana is grown, how it helps people, and how it's sold, you will be better able to understand the needs, opportunities, and role your brand idea or concept might fulfill.

Let's get you started on understanding your strengths so you know where your talents and passions will best fit. I've used a behavioral assessment tool, called the DiSC assessment, with clients for years. Its results serve as a type of owner's manual. You can go online and find a free version of the DiSC assessment, or you can pay to take the official one and get the full report on your results (I recommend that you pay for the full assessment to get the gritty details).

The DiSC assessment is a psychological tool designed by psychologist William Marston and further developed by Walter Clarke. It tests for four different behavior types:

- Dominance
- Influence
- Submission/Steadiness
- Compliance/Conscientious

These behavior types came from people's sense of self and their interaction with their environment (one of the reasons we already spent time on your pain and your experiences). The test has developed over time and is grounded in sound evidence that gives people an accurate understanding of themselves. DiSC is a tool to get to know yourself and how you deal with situations where interpersonal relationships are involved. It can help define your leadership skills. Different leadership methods and styles coincide with each personality type, and they can help leaders be more effective. There are no "bad" or "good" results. Most versions of the test will tell you that you align with one of the fifteen personality types based on the four major behavior types. You will also find out if you are predominantly D, i, S, or C in your behaviors:

- Achiever
- Agent
- Appraiser
- Counselor
- Creative
- Developer
- Inspirational
- Investigator
- Objective Thinker
- Perfectionist
- Persuader
- Practitioner
- Promoter
- Result-oriented
- Specialist

Once you have your information, read the following descriptions of each major type and the fields in the marijuana industry that might best align with your strengths. Don't feel limited by this. Rather, let it give you an idea of the direction you might lean. Each of us has all four of these personalities, just in varying degrees and with varying preferences. Use your results as a guide only.

DOMINANCE (D) — THE LEADER[1]

When the chips are down, people turn to you. You're forceful, decisive, and no-nonsense. You want results and you want

1 Descriptions for all four personality types from: https://www.collegerecruiter.com

them now. You don't have much patience for dilly-dallying or for anything that falls short of your high standards. Basically, you're CEO material. However, these traits also have a dark side. For example, when you are too focused on results, you risk railroading over the people who helped you get those results in the first place. If you're not careful, you will develop a reputation as a cold, unapproachable person who cares more about how people benefit you than the people themselves. They may put up with you as long as you get things done, but the moment you fail ... well, let's just say they won't let you live that down.

Ideal jobs: manager, department head – any job that makes the best use of your formidable leadership skills.

Cannabis industry jobs: dispensary or franchise owner, associated business owner, grow production manager.

INFLUENCE (I) – THE CHARMER

You are a people person. You genuinely enjoy the company of others and they return the favor. The mere sight of you vaporizes any tension in the office because you go out of your way to chat with people and make them feel good about themselves and their work. If your company had a Mr./Ms. Congeniality award, you'd probably win it. Sometimes though, you take your closeness with people a little too far. You don't think twice about gossiping behind someone's back if it means getting into someone else's good graces. Also, you often use your gift of gab to get out of trouble – the kind of trouble that would've been avoided if you didn't give in to your foot-in-mouth tendencies in the first place.

Ideal jobs: salesperson, public relations officer – any job that requires networking and dealing with people within a fast-paced environment.

Cannabis industry jobs: any type of manager, any cannabis service business.

STEADINESS (S) – THE PEACEKEEPER

You are the proverbial glue that holds the group together. Like the Charmer, you genuinely like people, but you express this by maintaining cordial relationships with your co-workers, rather than pumping them up with motivational speeches and jokes. You are patient, attentive, and reliable; of the four types, you are the one who is least likely to rock the boat, so to speak. There is nothing egregiously wrong with you – which is both a good and a bad thing. You're just so okay with everything and so unwilling to go against the status quo that memorable is the last word people think of when describing you. When faced with conflict, you do everything in your power to keep it from escalating, even if it's at your expense.

Ideal jobs: human resource officer, business process specialist – any job that makes use of your exceptional relational skills and attention to law and order.

Cannabis industry jobs: customer service manager, client relationship manager, dispensary manager, real estate.

CONSCIENTIOUSNESS (C) – THE THINKER

You're an idea person. You have the same drive to meet high standards as the Leader does, but you're not as interested in handling people. In fact, you'd rather work alone, and if pressed to make a decision on behalf of a group, you would rather gather all the facts first before you say anything. Because of this, you are prone to analysis paralysis. You also have trouble communicating your ideas to others since you are more concerned with precision than clarity. When things go wrong, you crack and automatically blame yourself for it, even if other forces are at play. Like the worst type of Leader, you risk coming across as a robot in human skin every time you fail to factor the human element into your daily interactions and decisions.

Ideal jobs: accountant, programmer – any job that requires rigorous analysis and independent work.

Cannabis industry jobs: grow manager, grow master, grower, electrician, plumber, HVAC expert.

In addition to your DiSC results and the work you did in the Get Real section, please use this set of questions that blend personal understanding with professional goals to further unpack what path you might take (answering the two core questions of this chapter: What are my personal strengths? What are my professional strengths and weaknesses?):

- What do I care most about?

- What makes me uniquely qualified to be successful? What am I bringing that no one else can?

- What impact am I passionate about having through my work?

- Do I live to work, work to live, or something in the middle? (This should inform the personal time investment that different branches of this industry require.)

- How do I like to spend my time? (What is fulfilling? What is fun?)

- What are my least favorite ways to spend my time? (What wears you out? What do you dislike?)

- What motivates me?

- Who are some of my business heroes? Why?

- Do I prefer structured or unstructured time?

- Do I prefer working alone or with others?

- Do I prefer working alongside or leading?

- Do I prefer consulting/individual service relationships or do I like being a part of an everyday organization?

- Do I prefer to specialize or do I like to be a jack-of-all-trades?

- Do I prefer spending my time interacting with people or with plants/systems/etc.?

- Do I want to run my own business? If so, what are the biggest risks for me?

- What is my current financial situation (assets vs. liabilities)?

- What technical skill sets do I already have?

- What professional experiences do I already have?

Here is a list of common paths in this industry that will help you begin aligning your personal and business answers you just provided, with what you may want to pursue:

- Grower
- Trimmer
- Dispensary Owner
- Marketing Specialist
- Real Estate Agent
- Electrician
- Plumber
- HVAC Technician/Business Owner
- Builder/Project Manager for Grow Build-Outs
- Lawyer
- CPA
- IT
- Extractor
- Cook
- Budtender
- Architect
- Political Liaison
- Transportation
- Compliance Officer
- Security
- HR ... and on and on

Take time to describe what your ideal role in this industry will be based on your new (or deepened) self-awareness:

_____

_____

_____

_____

_____

_____

_____

_____

_____

_____

_____

_____

_____

_____

_____

_____

_____

_____

I believe that this world is filled with an abundance of opportunities, and there are a lot of good people out there to take advantage of them. I want you to choose the opportunity that will elevate and take advantage of the BEST of who you are.

DREAM ON

AEROSMITH

Naming Path-Specific Goals

NOW WE'VE GOTTEN CLEAR ON HOW you carefully approach blending passion and business, what you want out of this experience through your impact (what you might do with the money), what your strengths are, and what aspect of this industry will allow you to balance and align all of this most effectively. In the spirit of creating a clear vision so that the voice in your head is driving you in the right direction, the rest of this section is about getting clear on your goals.

One of my favorite questions to ask is, "What would you attempt if you knew you couldn't fail?"

Think about it for a minute. Maybe you're not like me, but in the past, I used to hedge my dreams. I would say something silly like, "It would be great to have this and that, or to be able to do this or that, but … a private jet? Probably not."

Why not? What does the term realistic mean? You hear it all the time from naysayers – "That's not realistic," "Stop daydreaming," or "Get your head out of the clouds."

Fuck those people. DREAM ON!!

I'll share two "crazy" ones that I have. One, I'd like to have enough money to own a Nascar Racing Team and then insist that I'm the driver. Why not? Who the hell wouldn't want to watch those races just to see what an outsider can do? People are always talking about the problems with Formula 1 and its diminishing popularity. If it's not NASCAR, maybe Formula 1 needs a regular guy like me to give it a try. And second, I'd love to convince an NFL owner to hire me as the head coach. Can you imagine watching a team that never punted the ball, ever (because that would be one of my rules)? Or a team with a simplified play book so there were fewer mistakes and better fundamentals? It's just entertainment, but we take it way too seriously. If ten children could be cured of cancer if a certain team won the game, I'd root for that team all day, but in the end, it's just a game. It seems like we've elevated NFL players akin to Neil Armstrong or da Vinci or something, yet these are just talented people playing a game. You might be thinking, "Dude, those dreams actually are crazy." Maybe, but I have a lot of fun with it and why can't we have fun when we dream?

I'm sure J.K. Rowling got a lot of flak from people when she was on welfare and writing a book about a bunch of kids that could do magic … we know how that worked out. Let those big dreams, the ones that seem impossible from where you are today, out of your mind and put them down on paper. Then start working backward and build them into your plans. Goal setting is one of the most important things you can do for one main reason: something written down cannot easily be manipulated or brushed aside. If you only *say* something, it can be remembered wrong, forgotten, or changed. When you write something down, you can see there is independent documentation and accountability for the steps and the results. It's not just happening, or not happening, in your head.

Martin Luther King Jr. has a great quote that needs to be pointed out when considering these things. He said, "The ultimate measure of a man [/woman] is not where he [/she] stands in moments of comfort and convenience, but where he [/she] stands in times of challenge and controversy."

Look, if you've been around enough, you have probably been ripped off a few times, had your heart broken one or five times, lost out on something you really, really wanted, or even been roughed up a little. Starting a business, especially one in this industry, will require getting through some tough days. You know that. The things that will keep you focused, directed, and positive during those tough days are the things you've set out in your reflections, and a clear vision of the goal you're trying to reach. It is a long game. Having said that, here are a few questions to get you thinking, given your idea for where you fit in this industry and what you hope to earn:

Where do you want to be in five years? Ten years? Twenty-five years?

What big "unrealistic, crazy, no-one-thought-I-could-do-it" things do you want out of this?

Based on your thoughts about those questions, write at least three BIG goals for yourself. The best goals are SMART (specific, measurable, achievable, relevant, and timely). The more detailed you can be about your vision, the more real it will seem. If a vehicle is in your future, what specific vehicle are you going to be driving? What color? What year? What are you going to be wearing that first time you drive it? Who are you doing it with? Where are you going? Etc.

Example: I will start and own the most profitable dispensary in the city within three years of opening, with revenues of at least _____, and a reputation for having the best customer experience anywhere.

- _____
  _____
  _____
  _____

- _____
  _____
  _____
  _____

- _____
  _____
  _____
  _____

CARRY THAT WEIGHT

THE BEATLES

Grounding in Motivation and Desire

AS YOU PREPARE TO WRITE YOUR PERSONAL declaration in the final chapter of this section, I want to be sure you deeply understand the difference between information and motivation. There is a fascination with knowing things and getting access to information (think about how often you look something up on your phone). Information, unfortunately, is overrated. Why? Because there is more information available to us now than at any time in history, and we are still wasting money and energy on things that get us no closer to our goals or to achieving happiness. This book gives you a lot of information – and it is important. As I said, knowledge of your field is a must for success. However, your WHY is the driver that motivates you to apply the information that will really determine your outcome.

Let's talk through an example. According to LIVESTRONG, the obesity rate among adults in 1950 was 10 percent, and in 2017 that rate increased to 35 percent. How can that be? We know more than ever about weight loss and weight management. We know that there are two ways to control your weight: what you eat (calorie intake) and exercise (calorie burning). We know that if you need 1,500 calories to exist, and you eat 2,500 calories without burning those extra 1,000 calories during that day, you will store those calories and gain weight. If it's that simple, and we have all the information, then why are we less healthy than we have ever been in America?

The reason is that many people's relationship to food and exercise has nothing to do with what they know, and everything to do with how they feel. It has to do with their pain, their experiences, and ultimately their actions. Many businesses have figured this out, and take advantage of it with unbelievable profit. According to the website *Fooducate* and its article, "The Weight Loss Industry by Numbers," Americans spend $60,000,000,000 to lose weight every year (that's $60 billion dollars). At any given time, 75 million Americans are actively trying to lose weight. About $3 billion dollars is spent on weight-loss chains such as Weight Watchers. Another $3 billion is spent on diet pills and meal-replacement solutions.

You get the point. People who most successfully manage their weight and health usually do it by working on the root cause of whatever their weight problem actually is, so that they can tap into lasting solutions for their health, and understand more deeply why they want to be healthier: their why.

In this book, I am providing the right information and plan, but ask you to tap into your desire and motivation by becoming more self-aware and creating a clear vision for what you want and why you want it. Use me and our company to help you stay motivated, but never lose sight of the fact that your action will be the difference-maker in your ability to shift gears and be successful in a new field. Some of you will be able to take this information and start applying it today. If that's you – great. Some of you have the desire to produce results, but you don't have the correct information. Some of you will need, or want, support through the process to get you all the way to success. I do not want this to be a book that sits on your shelf collecting dust. I want this to be the opening for you to fulfill your destiny.

GET EDUCATED

THE BUSINESS — THE SETUP

THE CORE

ERIC CLAPTON

Mission Statement and Values

FOR ALL OF YOU IMAGINING A PATH THROUGH this industry that involves owning any kind of business or running any kind of service (I'd imagine that's most of you), you need to have a way to communicate to internal and external stakeholders what you're all about. You also need something that guides your business decisions to ensure you stay aligned to your original purpose. Just like your personal declaration and goals, a mission statement and strong set of values are the core that will keep you grounded and inspired in your work. It offers those who follow you clarity around how you want to do business, and it gives customers a sense of what they can expect if they choose you. Your mission and values should be the "railroad tracks" of the business: the clear and easy-to-follow path for all involved.

MISSION STATEMENT

The mission statement should be clear, simple, and name the fundamental aspiration of the business. It plays a huge role in creating the identity of your business. You may want to consider engaging partners or employees in the creation of the mission statement, as the more people are invested in it, the more likely it will become a reality.

To get started, brainstorm around the following questions regarding your business:

What do we do?

_____

_____

_____

_____

_____

How do we do it?

_____

_____

_____

_____

_____

Who do we serve?

_____

_____

_____

_____

_____

_____

What is special about how we serve people?

_____

_____

_____

_____

What difference do we make, and why does it matter to us?

_____

_____

_____

_____

The mission statement should communicate the *what* and the *why* of your business (values will guide the *how*). Use your answers to the previous questions and create one for yourself. I've included my own mission statement, as well as those of several well-known institutions, as examples for you.

Weedonomics

Weedonomics catalyzes positive transformation in the lives of people committed to maximizing their potential and impact in the cannabis industry and beyond.

Stanford Business School

Our mission is to create ideas that deepen and advance our understanding of management and with those ideas to develop innovative, principled, and insightful leaders who change the world.

Google

Organize the world's information and make it universally accessible and useful.

Yours:

_____

_____

_____

_____

_____

_____

If you've written a mission statement that you truly believe in, you can trust that mission statement to provide guide rails for you when things are tough. You can always ask yourself: What will move me toward my mission? Which option is in service of my mission? How will this decision impact my mission? Since you can't always be present with every employee, investing them in the mission and showing them how to act in service of it will also help your people make good decisions in your absence.

You want to be working on the business, not in the business. Think System.

There is no doubt that publicizing a mission statement puts you on the hook to pursue it in all that you do. People won't follow a leader whose words and actions don't align, so choose a statement that will push you to think and act at your best, and be sure you absolutely believe in it.

VALUES

Values provide the same compass to you and your employees as the mission statement does, but they become the "how" for doing business the way you want to. Earlier, you read Stanford Business School's mission. Concerning values, they say, "Our values provide the context within which the school strives for excellence." They list their values as follows:

- **Engage intellectually**
- **Strive for something great**
- **Respect others**
- **Act with integrity**
- **Own your actions**

You can see how, if everyone in that community is living by these values, the mission will be realized. Values can be short statements or simply words. The important thing is that you, and everyone you expect to live the values, know what they mean.

Here are my values and definitions, and explanations of why I chose them:

Respect: Treat everyone with dignity.

Responsibility: Be accountable for what you do.

Integrity: Be truthful. Do what you say.

Humility: Nothing gets accomplished alone.

Service: Be of assistance, be beneficial, serve others.

Passionate: Be enthusiastic about the life you live.

Effort: Be vigorous and determined.

Respect is first because everyone deserves a basic level of respect, and there has to be respect in order to allow all values to be heard. If you don't respect someone and they feel that, they won't care to hear anything you have to say. As it is my aspiration to guide people in transforming their opportunity, I need – and I need everyone in my company – to show people the utmost respect for their courage to make a change.

Responsibility means that I/we own what we do/did. If I say I'm going to do something, I do it. That simple. Nothing gets done in the entrepreneurial space if you can't follow through.

Integrity is essential for maximum effectiveness of any entity. If you do not do what you say, you have no credibility and a weakened reputation. When people can't trust you, it's over – the relationship, that is.

Humility is important because I believe no one is an island. People have helped me all along the way. I believe we are connected and need each other as human beings.

Service is at the heart of my company. We exist to serve. Some think that being gentle and kind are signs of weakness, but to me, it is the exact opposite. It takes strength, effort, energy, and thoughtfulness to be of service.

Passionate and enthusiastic is just me, so it's easy for me to live this value, but I also believe that if today could be my last day, I'm going to go out strong.

Effort is essential for success. It is often the little things that make the biggest difference. I believe in making an effort to show people how big your heart is.

Here is a long list of words, any of which could be a value in your business. Go through them and circle any that particularly resonate with you. Then place all the circled words in prioritized order depending on how central you believe them to be to your mission. Next choose the ones you want to put into action. If you have more than ten, you need to narrow it down even more.

Acceptance	Cooperation	Equality
Accomplishment	Courage	Ethics/ethical
Achievement	Create	Excellence
Acquisition	Creativity	Experience
Adventure	Danger	Experiment
Alignment	Dare	Expertise
Altruism	Delight	Explain
Amusement	Dependability	Exquisiteness
Assistance	Detection	Facilitation
Attractiveness	Dignity	Fairness
Authenticity	Direct	Faith
Awareness	Discovery	Fame
Beauty	Discrimination	Family
Being	Distinguish	Feeling good
Bliss	Diversity	Fitness
Calm	Economic security	Freedom
Charity	Education	Friendship
Coach	Effectiveness	Fun
Community	Elegance	Generosity
Compassion	Emotional well-being	Grace
Comprehending	Empathy	Gratitude
Connection	Encourage	Guidance
Consciousness	Encouragement	Happiness
Consideration	Energy	Harmony
Constancy	Enlightenment	Health
Contentment	Entertainment	Honesty
Contribution	Environment	Honor

Hope
Humility
Imagination
Improvement
Independence
Influence
Information
Inner peace
Innovation
Inspiration
Instruction
Integrity
Intelligence
Inventiveness
Joy
Justice
Kindness
Knowledge
Laughter
Leadership
Learning
Love
Loyalty
Magnificence
Mastery
Merriment
Nobility
Nurturance
Observation
Order
Organization
Originality

Peace
Peacefulness
Perception
Personal development
Play
Pleasure
Positive attitude
Power
Preparation
Presence
Proficiency
Provider
Quest
Radiance
Recognition
Relatedness
Relationships
Relaxation
Reliability
Religion
Resourcefulness
Respect
Responsibility
Responsiveness
Risk
Safety
Schooling
Self-awareness
Self-worth
Sensations
Sensuality
Serenity

Service
Simplicity
Spirituality
Stability
Stimulation
Strength
Strengthen
Success
Superiority
Support
Teaching
Tenderness
Touch
Tranquility
Trust
Truth
Truthfulness
Understanding
Victory
Vision
Wealth
Wholeness
Winning
Wisdom

Next, look up the definition of each word you have chosen, and frame a statement from that baseline describing how these values apply to your mission and work.

_____

_____

_____

_____

_____

_____

_____

_____

_____

_____

_____

_____

_____

_____

_____

_____

_____

_____

_____

Have you ever seen those "what's different?" books? My son loves them. Two pages are extremely similar, with subtle differences. Your job is to find the differences. What is interesting to me is that when looking at it from three feet away, they are the same. When you get close, they are different. I find the same to be true about people. We are mostly similar, and yet it seems fashionable to lead with our differences. I find it puzzling. I personally strive to find common ground with as many people as possible to get connected with others. Seek to find common ground with people, and you will find better and deeper relationships wherever you are. Hopefully, your values provide a common "language" that feels inviting to employees and customers alike, and – when they look closer – your mission statement will tell them what is special and different about you and your business.

EAZY-ER SAID THAN DUNN

EAZY-E

Live Your Mission and Values

IT IS WONDERFUL AND INSPIRING TO TALK about mission statements and values, and it feels good to write them down, but living them, doing the work all the time, is easier said than done. As a leader, if your employees, investors, customers, or others don't see you aligned to your mission and living your values, they *will* hold it against you. Customers will even hold it against you if your employees aren't doing the same. Making a commitment to follow your mission and live your values is no small thing, and you have to take it seriously. It's been said that our children are watching us with a record button on at all times, and it's true. We as a society have never been more tracked, photographed, or recorded than at any time in history, and it's not just at home; it's everywhere. A good internal thought would be: "Is what I'm saying or doing right now something I want to broadcast to the world?" If not – stop. Instead, say or do things with integrity.

People have very little forgiveness for leaders whose actions and words do not align or whose words do not align with their stated values and beliefs. Counter to the popular phrase, "Talk is cheap," talk can also come at a great cost for any leader who talks carelessly. You can spend a lifetime doing great work, helping many people and being an all-around good citizen, and then have it tainted by the "internet mob" in moments. Here's an image to remind you of this idea: as one apple ripens, it produces a gaseous hormone called ethylene, which is a ripening agent. The riper an apple is, the more gas it produces. This is nature's signal to other apples on the tree. However, when a bunch of apples are piled together, the gas from this one apple can cause the whole bunch to over-ripen and eventually rot. This is where the phrase, "One bad apple can spoil the whole bunch" comes from. The same can happen to leaders. Our public image is created of a "bunch" of what people have seen and heard from us, and even one bad statement, one foolish comment, one questionable post, can poison and rot all other work. I believe that we are never as bad as our worst mistake (key word: mistake), but generally, human beings don't give each other the benefit of the doubt and don't take time to seek out evidence to disprove a negative impression.

Consider the story of Jimmy "the Greek" Snyder, a man whose story takes place before the internet craze. Jimmy Snyder was an uneducated gambler who got his first huge win betting $10,000 on Truman to win the 1948 presidential election (the odds were 17 to 1). He moved to Las Vegas and created a sports line that eventually led to a twelve-year stint on the CBS Sunday morning show, *The NFL Today*, a pregame show for National Football League games. He used his limited background to become a star and make a ton of money. He was rough around the edges, but most people seemed to enjoy him and his style. Jimmy had also gone through a devastating personal history. He and his wife had lost three of their five children to cystic fibrosis, and he had continued on despite this tragedy. He was, by all accounts, successful. Then, in 1988, he commented to a reporter over dinner and drinks that "African-Americans were naturally superior athletes, at least in part, because they had been bred to produce stronger offspring during slavery." When it went public, he was immediately remorseful and said it was a foolish thing to say. A famous African-American athlete who knew Snyder came to his defense, saying he did not think Snyder was racist, and one sports reporter said that Snyder often tried to sound more educated than he was, so he said things he knew nothing about, and sometimes didn't believe. Regardless, his career was over. What he said was terrible and saying it went against his image of being a famous "average Joe," just one of the people. It didn't matter that Jimmy and others repeatedly professed it did not represent his true opinion. The powers that be couldn't get past it. This guy had come up from nothing and built an empire around him, but it all came crashing down around a too-casual and vastly inappropriate comment. Just one. More recently, also see Roseanne Barr and Megyn Kelly.

This is obviously an extreme example, and I hope none of you would find yourself in this type of position, but this can happen after much less inflammatory comments. As you prepare for true leadership, you must up your self-awareness around how you live (and speak and type) your values in service of your mission. Simply put, before you hit send or "pop off" on a post, don't pull a Greek.

THE RULER'S BACK

JAY-Z

Business Plans

THE BEST OUTCOMES IN LIFE ARE USUALLY DERIVED from a plan of some sort, even if it's a very simple plan. In the case of starting your own business, you must have a plan – and not a simple one, but a detailed one. It is one of the most important steps to creating a successful and lasting business. We use rulers (measuring tapes, levels, etc.) when building something because they are exact. When you know specifically how you plan to measure something, you can more accurately assess if you've accomplished what you intended. Your business plan, which will outline your desired outcomes and the path that will guide you there, provides the ruler to your success. The more specific you get in your plan, the clearer you will be as to how you are measuring against your desired results. You are intentionally building something, not winging it.

One convenient way to work through a business plan is by using available software programs built just for this purpose. This method can be great because it asks questions and prompts thinking about things that you may not have considered. You can search for available programs and pricing that feel right for you, but here is information to get you started.

It is a common misconception that business plans are written mainly to raise funding. A business plan is really written to be the blueprint of the business from inception to future success. Good business plans include careful thinking and research into obstacles, and plans for those eventualities, so the owner doesn't get stuck along the way. If a business plan is done really well, it also can be used to provide information to investors, an opportunity for them to assess the strengths and weaknesses of your plan, and identify possible opportunities and return on investment. Keep in mind: many investors will look at your plan as much to see that you are a sound thinker and leader as to assess the business itself.

To begin, every business plan should answer four central questions:

- What are you going to do?
- How will you apply your qualifications/strengths to ensure your success?
- What is the competition, and what will make you better than the competition?
- How will you make money?

Here are the key elements of the business plan:

- *Executive Summary:* The story about your business and the opportunity, in two pages or less.
- *Business Overview:* The mission statement, vision, values, products, and uniqueness you deliver, and the opportunity available.
- *Business Environment (Market Analysis):* An analysis of the marketplace, customers, competition, and what makes your solution unique.
- *Organizational Structure:* How your business will be structured and the people involved.
- *Strategy:* The roadmap to success. How your business addresses the business environment (including marketing).
- *Financials:* A built-out cash flow statement and financial forecasts/projections for your expenses and revenue.
- *Action Plan:* Implementation steps with benchmarks and goals for how you will achieve your stated outcomes/financial forecast.

If you own a dispensary, you will encounter the need to plan for three different types of businesses in one: manufacturing, retail, and service.[1]

Manufacturing questions to consider:

- Where is the best grow location?
- What systems will I use for seed-to-sale tracking?
- Who will I use as suppliers for my grow room and necessary products? Where are they located?

---

[1] *The Sales sections will also inform elements of your plan you should consider.*

- From where will I supply my original seeds/clones?
- Will I be making more than one product?
- How will I manage the product?
- How will I manage inventory?
- What procedures do I have in place for security? Employee theft?
- Where will I find the most qualified growers, and what training do I need to do for the growers?
- How will I address quality control for my plants?
- Will I manage my own grows or will I hire a manager?

Retail questions to consider:
- How will I strategically determine my location and design my store layout?
- Will I rent or purchase my property?
- How will I market? What will my business name be?
- How can I use technology and social media to my benefit?
- How do I hire great employees? What will make for great employees? What training will they need?
- Will I manage my own dispensary, or will I hire a store manager?
- Will I manage my own finances, or will I hire an accountant/CPA?

Service questions to consider:
- What markets will I serve, and what are their specific needs? Where are my customers located?
- How will people experience my store, from location to layout to sale?

- How will I apply the sales and service systems I now understand?
- How will I get positive reviews publicized?
- How will I collect and resolve customer complaints and/or frustrations?
- How will I empower my employees to solve problems for the store and for customers?

Once you're up and running, here are the top seven warning signs that your plan is not working and that you should go back to your plan to make adjustments.

- *You are not making any money (profits).* Go back to your financials and see what is happening. Financial problems are not always simple, but you can always get expert advice on how you're managing them. You already know that complex problems cannot be solved overnight, and ignoring or pretending that they are not there will just get you in a worse situation. You will make mistakes, and you might even, dare I say, be wrong from time to time. When this happens, pivot your position to achieve success. If you are willing to stay aware and responsive, you can almost always recover. Remember, Microsoft came up with the concept of a computer on every desk at home, and MISSED the next logical step, which was a phone in every hand. As you well know, Apple capitalized on the second idea, but Microsoft still found a way to recover and move forward.

- *You were doing well, sales were high, and then they started to fall.* If you were doing well and now you are not, there must be a reason. It is usually a disconnect between what you think you are offering and what your customers expect or experience. A new competitor could be taking business from you, or it could be a major breakdown in service. Start hanging around the store and see what is happening. Also, hire a mystery shopper or have a friend shop the store and give you feedback. Make sure your financial health is where it needs to be as you've grown, and that you are still wisely balancing your costs with your revenue.

- *You are not meeting your financial forecasts.* As you are creating your plan, make two forecasts. One forecast should be aggressive, envisioning that everything goes extremely well. The second should be more conservative. Once you're up and running, be sure you aren't falling below the conservative forecast, but accept that you may end up somewhere between the two. The main idea here is: don't ignore the numbers.

- Competitors are driving numbers down. Just to give you an idea, in the Denver metro area there are:
  - 31 McDonald's locations
  - 80 Starbucks locations
  - 169 Medical dispensaries
  - 195 Recreational dispensaries

Stay on top of what is happening in your retail universe. These are obviously high numbers, but the demand is high, too. As you plan, consider your locations carefully, and do your market research – both what the markets currently are, and where markets may be developing. When this industry gets opened up federally (and it will), companies with big money behind them will try to get involved and dominate the market. There will be closures and disruptions. This is why I'm stressing system, system, system, and people, people, people. You need to be stable in this industry as quickly as you can so you stay competitive. I've included a chapter on pricing, but be sure you don't fall into the trap of simply trying to lower prices. There are other ways to recapture business that don't eat into your profit margin: more detailed market research, outreach to adjust services, premium services and products, and doubling down on referral systems ... to name a few.

- *The market shifts under you (and it will).* If you remember, people used to go to a store called Blockbuster and rent movies. You may have heard that a concept similar to Redbox (a self-service movie rental kiosk) was offered to senior management at Blockbuster, and they passed on it. Then the market shifted into technology and internet-based movies, and Netflix ate Blockbuster up. Blockbuster went bankrupt. Pay attention to new ideas and stay open to change (like Blockbuster should have).

- *Your people are unhappy.* Hopefully, this will not happen to you after you read this book because you will be a self-aware leader who aligns words and actions to your stated values and mission. Remember, the only interaction your customers have is with your employees. If employees are unpleasant or rude because they are unhappy, it will obviously hurt your bottom line. For example, I hired a contractor who has a large company. Toward the end of the project, I told our foreman that they had neglected to take care of a few things we had agreed on. In response, a guy I had never met sent me an email that essentially called me a liar. Clearly, he was defensive, and probably under a lot of stress, but that one email damaged my relationship with the company after a year of working with them. There is too much competition in this business. You cannot lose customers due to employee dissatisfaction. Take. Care. Of. Your. People.

- *The best problem to have, but still a problem: You are growing really fast and can't quite keep up.* There is so much growth in this industry that it can be hard to keep up with the level of product quality you want, and you are running at 100 mph all the time. Your attention will be split across many components of your business, and you need to be sure you prioritize the right things given your strengths, and delegate other items to employees you trust and train. As with our last problem, you don't want the customer experience to suffer. You have likely heard the claim: If you have a happy customer, they will tell one person, and if you have an unhappy customer, they will tell ten people. With social media, this statement has been magnified both positively and negatively – you want to count on positive publicity.

No business problem cannot be solved by leveraging the right resources. If you need more people, revisit your finances and figure out how to get them, train them, and pay them (not to mention keep them). If you need more product, expand your grow. Be nimble, get help, and respond quickly.

(I'LL GIVE YOU) MONEY

PETER FRAMPTON

Funding Your Business

SPEAKING OF LEVERAGING YOUR RESOURCES, you are going to need some to get started. If your idea and plan for your business is the engine, then money is the fuel that powers the engine and keeps it running. If you want to start a dispensary or any business related to this industry, you need to consider how to fund your endeavor.

Here are eleven common ways business owners raise money, and the advantages and disadvantages of each:

- Crowdfunding
- Angel Investors
- Venture Capital
- Partners

- Small Business Administration (SBA) Loan
- Commercial Loan or Line of Credit
- Bank Loan
- Home Equity Line of Credit (HELOC)
- Credit Cards
- Family and Friends
- You

11. CROWDFUNDING

This is an excellent way to test the market. There are many tips and videos on how to produce a great campaign.

Advantages: You get to test your idea with the masses before risking all, or any, of your own money. The willingness of a large group to make micro-investments suggests you may also have a good market of possible customers. You also get to inspire people with your great idea and have them participate in seeing it come to life. Many times, there is a "gift" or promise of a completed product for the investor to receive. The biggest advantage is that if your idea doesn't fly, you don't have to pay anyone back, and you are not out much of your own money.

Disadvantages: With crowdfunding, you give up some control because you've shared your idea very publicly in its current state. You also might lose time while drumming up the money you need. Finally, your concept is exposed, and others could use it as their own if you are not legally protected. To get the funding, you would likely have to "sell" people on your unique approach/edge/idea, and that exposes your thinking to your competition.

10. ANGEL INVESTORS

Angels generally take on more risk than venture capital (VC) firms because they invest their personal money, while VCs have a portfolio of investments within the company. Angel investors are also more common while raising startup money in somewhat smaller amounts as opposed to VCs, which often invest further into the process and invest larger amounts.

Advantages: Angels are usually wealthy, so they have already done really well. They may share both money and their mentoring and experience. Angels are often willing to take greater risks, which allows you to move more quickly than traditional investors. They are individual investors, so you may find that they are also more patient about results because they are only answerable to themselves.

Disadvantages: If you don't like giving up a big piece of the pie to succeed, then this may not be the way for you. Angel investors expect good returns on their investments if you are successful, and also may look for a role in decision-making that could be unwelcome (unless you desire their involvement).

9) VENTURE CAPITAL

VCs are professional asset managers who work with groups of qualified investors seeking a high rate of return.

Advantages: If you need more money than a bank may lend you, or want to hedge what you borrow with someone else's money, you may like this option. Also, if you have a "bulletproof" business concept, management team, and ability to succeed, VCs are better set up than banks to take risks on good leaders and good plans. Some VCs also offer significant support to the businesses they invest in, and they have a lot of experience across different industries that they can offer you.

Disadvantages: In return for the money, VCs will take a major role in running the business, and a major ownership stake. You just have to be ready for this and want it, or it won't be a pleasant experience for you.

8) PARTNERS

Partners are people who have money, but no current business idea, or want the potential of a big return outside of typical investment opportunities.

Advantages: A partnership is usually designed to be fairly equal, meaning you both have something the other needs, and you both win if the business succeeds. It's more equal than the top-heavy VCs or angels.

Disadvantages: If the ground rules are not established in a partnership, written out clearly, and legally reviewed and authorized, things can get ugly quickly. You don't want any room for confusion in how you and your partner will engage in the work or the profits.

7) SMALL BUSINESS ADMINISTRATION (SBA) LOAN

The SBA loan is given out by a government agency to help small businesses that would have a difficult time traditionally funding a loan through a bank. It is a loan, not free, but because it is guaranteed, it helps get you funded.

Advantages: SBAs are a way that the federal government helps small businesses and takes the pressure off of you to fund yourself completely. Also, it is helpful to have other sets of professional funders' eyes on your business. This is where the holes will be punched in your plan.

Disadvantages: Did I mention it is a *federal government agency*? It is a long, long process to get through, and the first-time approval rate is 25 percent. As a loan, it obviously has to be paid back and managed.

6) COMMERCIAL LOAN OR LINE OF CREDIT

These loans are usually for established businesses, but they are a way to add on to what you are doing so you can draw from the line of credit when needed.

Advantages: You only pay interest on the money you use, kind of like a huge credit card. Smaller lines can be acquired collateral-free.

Disadvantages: It's a big credit card, it costs you to use it, and it eats into your profits. Also, larger credit lines may have to be secured with real estate, accounts receivable, inventory, and/or equipment, which means you could stand to lose resources you value if you can't make the payments.

5) BANK LOAN

This is just a traditional bank loan from a local branch. They consider your credit history, expertise, business experience, and of course, your business plan. They are trying to measure the likelihood that you'll succeed and take a more conservative lens than other funding sources.

Advantages: The main one is you keep all the equity in your business and have a few sets of eyes to test your plans through.

Disadvantages: You owe the money on time, every time, even if things don't go as planned. They share none of the risk with you, so they won't have sympathy if you run into problems. In other words, they are only financially invested; they aren't invested in helping you succeed.

4) HELOC

A home equity line of credit is a second mortgage on your home. If your house is worth $500K, and you owe $300K, then your equity is $200K. You can usually borrow money against this equity to get started.

Advantages: You have the money "sitting there." You are borrowing your own money, essentially, except you don't have to sell your house to access it. Again, you only pay interest on what you use, and if you do sell your house, this second loan, along with the principal mortgage (first), are automatically paid.

Disadvantages: You are putting your house, where you live with your family, in the mix. Are you prepared to lose your house if something goes wrong? Meaning, if your business fails and you lose that money, you are going to be making payments on that loan no matter what, and if you can't make them, you can go into foreclosure. Also, depending on the valuation of your home, that equity could vanish as the market changes.

3) CREDIT CARDS

Depending on what kind of business you are starting, credit cards could get you there. A credit card is a personally secured line of credit from a bank.

Advantages: You usually use a credit card for smaller amounts, and it's not connected to your home or other assets in any way. Often, the payments are lower than other types of loans. You also maintain all equity in your business.

Disadvantages: If you default on these loans, it could significantly damage your credit. Getting underwater with a credit card can happen fast, so be careful if you go in this direction.

2) FAMILY AND FRIENDS

Obvious.

Advantages: They know you (probably better than anyone else in the world), which is why it is tricky. The biggest advantage is the relationship. They want to be involved if they are talking with you about it, and they are more flexible and understanding than strangers. They love you, want you to live your dreams, and want to be a part of it. Does it get better than that? (Don't fuck this up.)

Disadvantages: Did I mention you don't want to fuck up these relationships? That is the biggest disadvantage. The last thing you want to feel when you see your family or friends is disappointment because of that "thing" that didn't work out, or worse, they think you outright ripped them off. Things can get weird around money very quickly. The last thing you want to do is damage personal relationships over money. I would NEVER take money from family and friends without everything being spelled out in great detail and put in writing.

Note: The real purpose of a written contract is this: At the beginning of any venture, everyone is always excited about how great it's going to be when ... The contract is there to keep things structured when it's not going well. It's like insurance. If you crash your car and people are injured, you are emotional and upset and they are emotional and upset. Insurance handles the details contractually because neither party is in a place to make good decisions in a crisis. Get things in writing before you start a business relationship with anyone, but especially family and friends.

1) YOU

Even more obvious. Savings, earnings, stocks, 401(k) funds, profits from real estate ... whatever you've got.

Advantages: It's all you! Your money, your vision, your plan, your work, your control, you own it, and it's all your money to spend.

Disadvantages: It's all you! Your money (lost), your vision (not realized), your plan (didn't work), your control (100 percent of the loss), you own it (and have no one to blame), and it's all your money to spend (and you spent it all).

... but that won't be you.

LEGALIZE IT

PETER TOSH

Legal Distinction

NOW THAT YOU HAVE A SOLID BUSINESS PLAN and you've made decisions about how you'll fund your business, you need to think about what type of legal entity you want your business to be. I answered the phone late in 2009, and it was a call that I'll never forget. It was a major bank in the US, and they were asking me for a payment of $25,000. I was stunned. You know that feeling? Your face gets hot and every little detail comes into focus. The main question was why. What in the hell was this person talking about? Then I thought, *well, there is no way this can be true,* so I tried to calm down. But I had to find out. The man told me I owed the money for a personal line of credit from 1997. This is what can happen to you if you do not set up your business correctly.

In 1997, I moved to Colorado to set up a business with a good friend. We didn't really know what we were doing, so we saved as much as we could, sold what we could, and then borrowed what we could. That amounted to about $50,000. We opened a retail store and got started. We were such good friends that while we formed an LLC (limited liability company) for the business, we didn't do it with much thought or follow-through. Then we opened a business account, secured personally, and used money from that to get started. Big mistake.

The problem was that over the years after we closed our business, my friend had used money from that line of credit and had spent it all. Then he went bankrupt. Since I was also on the account originally, even though I hadn't touched it in years, they called me to pay it. When he and I spoke about it, he swore that he asked the bank to take me off the account, and they never did. Having dealt with the banks intensely for many years, I believe him and we're still tight. In the end, I didn't have to pay, but needless to say, that caused a lot of bullshit. You obviously want to avoid that. I fully believe that he asked the bank to take me off the account, but they didn't because it is more beneficial for them to have more responsible parties. However, if we had set it up properly, then when we dissolved the company, everything related to it should have been dissolved, too. Choosing and thinking through your legal distinction is not just a formality to get through – be detailed and be aware of all the fine print.

Five ways you might get started:
- Sole Proprietorship
- Partnership
- Limited Partnership

- Limited Liability Company
- Corporation

SOLE PROPRIETORSHIP

A sole proprietorship is a business owned by a single person. It is the easiest type of organizational structure to adopt because there are no documents needed to begin the legal existence of a sole proprietorship.

Advantages: You have total control, 100-percent ownership, and it's easy to set up: no lawyers or complicated paperwork.

Disadvantages: The biggest one is the lack of liability protection. In essence, a creditor can pursue your personal assets to cure business debts in the case of bankruptcy.

PARTNERSHIP

A partnership is a type of business structure for you and one or more people.

Advantages: You are not in it alone. There is shared responsibly for management, obligations, and profits.

Disadvantages: You are not in it alone. Sometimes strong personalities or differing management styles and perspectives cause conflict that slows the progress of the business. Again, all partners can have their business and personal assets challenged as collateral if the company goes bankrupt. Having clear ground rules will make a monumental difference in the conflict realm, but won't solve the latter problem.

LIMITED PARTNERSHIP

A limited partnership can have one or more general partners and one or more limited partners.

Advantages: This is a good option for an investor who wants to have ownership and does not want to participate in day-to-day operations. They would only be liable to the extent of their investment.

Disadvantages: It can still get complicated with partners, or limited partners, without rock-solid ground rules in place.

LIMITED LIABILITY COMPANY (LLC)

An LLC is a combination of a corporation and a sole proprietorship or partnership.

Advantages: LLCs provide the personal asset protection of a corporation with the simplicity of a sole proprietor and partnership. It's the easiest way to get the maximum protection with the best ease of use. Taxation is another huge advantage. An LLC does not have to file a tax return as a business, as the company profits and losses pass directly on to a personal tax return.

Disadvantages: The cost of setup is the biggest drawback. Articles of organization and an operations agreement must be filed, and I highly recommend a lawyer does this for you. It can be expensive, but you don't want to mess up getting this right. For example, if someone sues you and claims that your LLC was not set up properly, you may not have the protections you anticipated, and could end up being personally liable.

CORPORATION

A distinct legal entity with a separate existence from shareholders of the business (think Coca-Cola, IBM, or GM).

Advantages: In a corporation, there is a limit on the liability of the owners. A shareholder's liability for company debts does not extend beyond what the shareholder invested.

Disadvantages: Since it is a separate entity (the Supreme Court has ruled that a corporation has the same legal rights as a human being), both the business and the owners are taxed separately. A corporation must file a corporate tax return and pay taxes on profits at the company's corporate tax rate. The second layer of tax occurs when dividends are distributed to shareholders. A shareholder must report dividends on one's personal income tax return and pay taxes on the dividends at the individual's personal income tax rate. Obviously, a lawyer would handle this, too. Again, there is something known as the "piercing of the corporate veil," meaning if you set up a corporation to do illegal things, you do not have the protections of the corporation. And if meetings and minutes are not held at the appropriate times, and recorded appropriately, you can also lose your protection.

I'm not a lawyer and I'm not giving legal advice, but I have chosen LLCs for the maximum protection and ease of setup and management. Remember, when you go big time, you can always convert your LLC to a corporation.

TRUTHS AND RIGHTS

JOHNNY OSBOURNE

Marijuana Industry Licensing

ONCE YOU'VE DECIDED ON THE LEGAL STRUCTURE of your business, you will also need to go through the process of ensuring you are properly licensed in this industry so that you are on the right side of the law. You also must ensure that your business is set up to meet the legal requirements outlined for the marijuana industry.[1]

This chapter is about truths, and your rights, concerning legal compliance in this industry. I'm going to speak about Colorado mainly, because things will change in your area quickly, and it would be a waste of time to try and incorporate all the different

---

[1] *Much of the information in this chapter is directly from the Colorado Department of Public Health and Environment website under the Medical Enforcement Division.*

states and rules here. However, many states are following Colorado's lead, so this information I am sharing, or a close variation of it, will likely be coming your way. I am going to give you an idea about how it all works.

Here is a list of items that will be of interest:

- What is seed-to-sale?
- How does someone get a Medical Marijuana Card?
- How do I get a Wholesale Grow License?
- What is the application process to get a Dispensary License?
- How do I get and renew my Occupational or Support License?
- What are the requirements to register as a Marijuana Caregiver/Cultivator or Transporter?

SEED-TO-SALE: WHAT IS IT AND HOW DOES IT WORK?

Seed-to-sale is a tracking system for marijuana plants from the beginning to the end of the process. Its main purpose is to stop illegal black market or gray market crimes. Black market is straight illegal growing and selling; gray market is growing marijuana in a state where it is legal to grow, and selling it in a state where it is not state legal. Having a strong seed-to-sale system is critical to the legality of your business if you are growing and/or running a dispensary.

Larry Alton talks about seed-to-sale and its importance in his *Huffington Post* article, "How Seed to Sale Systems Are Revolutionizing the Cannabis Industry." He explains how seed-to-sale software comes in many different forms, depending on the app you're using, but you need a system, and systems generally focus on these key areas:

- Barcodes. First, most seed-to-sale platforms rely on some type of barcode or other signature marker that can be automatically scanned at every point in the growth and distribution process. This includes literally every step of the process, as the name suggests, from the time a seed is planted to the point when the finished product makes it into customers' hands.

- Audit trails. One of the most important features for distributors is the availability of an audit trail, which they can produce if they're ever questioned by governmental authorities seeking proof that they're in compliance with the law. After logging in, they'll be able to access records dating back indefinitely for any product they grow or sell.

- Scales. Some seed-to-sale platforms have built-in digital scales, which integrate directly with the system. This allows distributors to make more precise measurements, and record those measurements for posterity.

- Strain analysis. There are thousands of different strains available, so it's sometimes hard to tell the difference. Giving a customer the wrong strain can be problematic on several levels, and if you're introducing a new strain, you'll want to track it to make sure it works as intended. Seed-to-sale platforms allow distributors to analyze the strains they produce and sell, streamlining this segment of the industry.

- Inventory management. Inventory management is crucial, both to maintain profitability and to improve the security of the operation. If marijuana inventory ever goes missing, it's a major problem.

- POS. Seed-to-sale platforms also come with a built-in point-of-sale (POS) system that allows customers to check out with a handful of simple prompts. It streamlines the checkout process, making life easier for customers, but also records and stores more data on every customer interaction. The fact that it's integrated with inventory management and audit trails makes it even more rewarding to the seller using the platform.

- Security. Most seed-to-sale platforms also have a heavy emphasis on security, preventing the handling or sale of products by anyone other than authorized staff members. More advanced platforms even have biometric technology that recognizes fingerprints and other physical signatures to restrict access.

Be sure you research what system you like the best, and understand most clearly. Having a seed-to-sale system in place can protect you from any allegations of misusing the product you grow and sell – an important part of this industry, especially while it is still not federally legal.

MEDICAL CARDS: HOW DO PEOPLE GET THEM?

Whether you want/need to be a medical card holder yourself, it will be important for you to understand these cards and how to advise customers seeking an understanding of them. Not only does this build trust with customers, but it also helps stabilize your customer base for medical product purchases. Here are the general guidelines (in Colorado) and information about the process.

Adults

To be eligible for a medical marijuana card, you must:

- Be a Colorado resident
- Be eighteen or older
- Have a qualifying medical condition

Minors

Minors are eligible for a medical marijuana card if:

- Minor and the primary parent are Colorado residents
- Minor has a qualifying medical condition

Qualifying medical conditions

- Cancer
- Glaucoma
- HIV or AIDs
- Cachexia
- Persistent muscle spasms
- Seizures
- Severe nausea
- Severe pain
- Post-Traumatic Stress Disorder (PTSD)

Look up your state's application online. Here is the Colorado site: https://www.colorado.gov/pacific/cdphe/how-apply-colorado-medical-marijuana-card

Here are a few tips to ease the successful completion of the application:

Adult applicants
- A valid Colorado ID or driver's license. If you are applying online, make sure to have a JPEG or PDF copy of your valid Colorado driver's license or ID. You will upload this to your registration.

- Caregiver's registration ID if you are applying with a caregiver.

- Credit card or bank account and routing number to pay your application processing fee.

Parents and legal representatives of minors
- Primary parent's Colorado driver's license or ID.

- If you are applying online, make sure to have a JPEG or PDF copy of the primary parent or legal representative's Colorado driver's license or ID. You will upload this to your registration.

- Certified copy of the minor's state-issued birth certificate.

- Caregiver's registration ID if parent is not the caregiver.

- Credit card or bank account and routing number to pay your application processing fee.

- Documentation to prove secondary parent status:
  - Secondary parent's out-of-state ID if parent lives out of state.

  - Certified copy of secondary parent's death certificate if parent is deceased.

  - Copy of court-issued sole custody order if secondary parent does not have any custody.

- Minor patient consent form.

Legal representatives of adults
- Patient's Colorado driver's license or ID.

- Legal representative's Colorado driver's license or ID.

- If you are applying online, make sure to have JPEG or PDF copies of the valid Colorado driver's licenses or IDs. You will upload these to your registration.

- Copies of legal representative documentation, medical power of attorney documents, or certified court orders.

- Caregiver's registration ID if the legal representative is not the caregiver.

- Credit card or bank account and routing number to pay your application processing fee.

WHOLESALE GROW LICENSE: WHY WOULD I WANT ONE, AND HOW DO I GET ONE?

The grower's license allows you to have a stand-alone recreational grow with no store equipment for medical licenses, and wholesale the product to any licensed recreational store or marijuana-infused product manufacturer in the state of Colorado. The initial fee for the license is $7,200. Eligible licenses can be applied for additional plant counts. Fees for extended plant counts could be $4,000–$8,000, depending on the size. General requirements include a clean background check with no outstanding tax or child-support debt. Like the medical marijuana card, you can look at your government site for the process. Here is the Colorado site: https://www.colorado.gov/pacific/enforcement/retail-marijuana-business-license-application

DISPENSARY LICENSE: HOW DO I GET ONE?

Before you decide if this is for you, it's important to know if you qualify (again, the information here is for Colorado). In Colorado, the Marijuana Enforcement Division (MED) regulates the process and applications to get an occupational license. One of the requirements is that you must be a Colorado resident.

Other requirements include:

- You must be twenty-one years old.

- You CANNOT have a felony conviction related to the possession, distribution, or use of any controlled substance.

- In the last five years, you must NOT have served probation, parole, or served a sentence of any felony offense.

- You cannot be a law enforcement officer.

- You cannot be the spouse or child or living in the same house as any employee of the MED.

- You cannot be a licensed physician making patient recommendations.

- You cannot have had your authority to act as a primary caregiver revoked by the state.

- You cannot be an officer or employee of the marijuana state licensing authority.

OCCUPATIONAL/SUPPORT LICENSE: WHAT ARE THEY AND HOW DO EMPLOYEES GET THEM?

The MED Occupational License allows the holder to work within MED-licensed medical and retail marijuana facilities or allows vendors to provide services to MED medical and retail marijuana business licensees. There are two types of MED Occupational Licenses, and both license types are good for two years from the date on which the license badge is issued:

- Key Employee (occupational): Necessary for employees that make operational or management decisions that directly impact the business. Example: a master grower that determines what or how much of a particular strain to produce. Application fee: $250

- Support Employee: Necessary for employees that

work within the business but do not make operational decisions. Example: a budtender. The majority of occupational license holders are in this category. Application fee: $75

Make sure your employees are properly licensed and that you keep those records at hand in your store locations. This is not a place to cut corners.

CAREGIVER/CULTIVATOR OR TRANSPORTER REGISTRATION: WHAT IS IT AND HOW DO I DO IT?

In Colorado, the MED requires four different types of people to register with the state:

- Cultivating: Grows marijuana on behalf of patients.

- Transporting: Transports marijuana for homebound or minor patients.

- Parents of a minor patient: Parents of a patient under age eighteen.

- Advising: Advises patients on the medicinal use of marijuana.

State statute requires that all Medical Marijuana Cultivating and Transporting Caregivers register the location of their Medical Marijuana Cultivation with the Department of Revenue.

Cultivating Caregivers must register:
- The location of each cultivation operation.

- The registration number of each patient for whom they cultivate medical marijuana.

- Any extended plant count numbers and their corresponding patient registry numbers (an extended plant count is any number greater than six).

Transporting Caregivers must register:
- The registration number of each homebound patient for whom they transport medical marijuana.

- The total number of plants and ounces that the caregiver is authorized to transport.

- If applicable, the location of each patient's registered medical marijuana center or caregiver cultivation.

Awareness of license legalities and what you need in your business will ensure that you are not putting yourself at risk in your state. It's tedious, and it's not the sexy part of this work, but make sure you get it done right.

CHANGES

DAVID BOWIE

Managing in a Changing Industry

THE LAST SEVERAL CHAPTERS IN THIS SECTION were meant to ensure that you set up a stable and lasting business. However, the marijuana industry is in a period of constant change, so you need to anticipate flexibility in your planning and ensure that you set up your business (including financially and legally) to change as gracefully as possible with industry movement.

Do you think if your business ordered 250,000 of something, and then couldn't use them, that it would affect your bottom line and cost you a lot of money? Of course it would. That is almost what happened to a Colorado company that makes marijuana-based drinks. This company went to the MED (Marijuana

Enforcement Division) to seek approval for an aluminum can design. The design had to have a clear side on the can with indicators for the serving size per can. The MED approved the design and the company ordered the cans. Then the MED came back and changed the design requirements. The company was potentially out 250,000 cans. The MED eventually allowed the company to use the cans because they had a written contract and followed the process correctly.

Now, if you completely dislike ch-ch-changes, this industry may not be for you ... yet. But these changes are why there is a huge opportunity here. It's like seeing a house with tremendous damage that needs to be rehabbed, or taking a dog from the shelter to turn its life around. When you are willing to do the work that most others will not, you get the greatest rewards.

Other states are also learning from Colorado, Washington, and California, so hopefully it will be smoother for you if you're exploring this field in a state that's just beginning. Regardless of where you are, you need to support your big dreams and goals with sound decisions and hard work. The good news is that agencies regulating this business are also figuring this out, so there is usually time to make adjustments when they are necessary.

WHAT'S YOUR NAME

LYNYRD SKYNYRD

Naming Your Business

OUR FINAL CHAPTER IN THIS SECTION IS – in my opinion – one of the most fun tasks in getting your business set up: picking out a name. It's a little like naming your children or your pets. It will be there forever: when you introduce it, in the logo, on your storefront, when someone writes a check to you, when you do your taxes … the name you pick will influence and dominate.

I chose the name Weedonomics after sifting through many names that didn't work (I had more than fifty on my list). I wanted to have something that, in one word, communicates what we're about and leaves you curious to know more. *Newsweek* had a title from a Collector's Edition magazine called *Weed 2.0*, and they probably spent a lot of money figuring out that "weed" was a word that people associated with the marijuana industry (which makes sense). Economics is the branch of knowledge concerned with the production, consumption, and transfer of wealth. People have heard the blending of words with economics like "Reaganomics," or more recently, "Trumponomics." The combination of weed and economics seemed to speak to what I wanted to communicate.

Here is a list of the top eight things you should consider when choosing a name:

- A name that is easy to pronounce. It seems simple, but I don't understand why you would want to make your potential customers try to figure out how to say your name, or have people mispronounce it and get corrected. You never want your customers to feel foolish, especially when saying the name of your damn business. Also, you don't want something that people have to explain. You want it to be simple enough and clever enough to stick.

- A name that you are happy to say, especially saying it loud and proud. I think of children's names again. You want your child to have a name that is clean to say and simple to understand. Have something you'd feel great saying when you are opening on the stock exchange.

- Avoid names that are difficult to spell. Keep it simple. Ideally, you want your business to be easy to find online. Even though one of the biggest search engines out there will correct people's spelling mistakes, you want people to find you on the first try.

- A name that is available. You don't want to spend hours and hours working on this and then find out that your idea is already registered with the Secretary of State. Ideally, the company name and the domain name will match. They don't necessarily have to, but they need to be close. You have probably noticed a lot of companies are adding words to their names or putting "try" or "buy" or "usa" in their domain names to get around this (nissanusa and BMWusa are examples).

- Don't pick out a name that is regionally limiting or not inclusive of everything you do. Think of Jeff Bezos' company – Amazon. Their first big product was online books. If they had named the company "OnlineBookMobile" instead of Amazon, the name would have limited the expansion (or necessitated a complicated change). Avoid something with your location like, "The Denver Pizza Experience" in case you end up moving beyond one location. Keep it universal. I am going to take Weedonomics worldwide.

- A name that has meaning. Some names of companies out there have nothing to do with their business, like Yahoo and Apple. These are harder and more expensive to brand because you have to educate people on what it is, and that takes time and money.

- Get feedback from people who will tell you the truth. I ran my name by more than a few people, and the one negative comment I got for my final choice was that it was "a little clunky." I liked the feedback but still decided it was right for me and what I was doing. There can be a ton of back and forth on this. In the end, you have to love saying it to people and have it check all the other boxes as well. Go with your gut, too. I think Yahoo is a silly name, but they have more money than me, so what the hell do they care what I think? You also want to avoid this scenario when possible: Buick named one of its vehicles the LaCrosse, apparently a word used in Quebec, Canada, as the slang term for masturbation (probably not what they were hoping for). In Spanish, Nova means "doesn't go" ... No Va. Not the best choice for the name of a Chevrolet car. Be sure your name doesn't mean something totally different somewhere else.

- Secretary of State and trademark search: Before you start designing a logo and picking out the colors, check with your secretary of state to see if the name is available, and run a check at the Unites States Patent and Trademark Office (USPTO.gov) to see if it is available to secure.

GET EDUCATED

THE BUSINESS — THE BASICS

SWEET EMOTION

AEROSMITH

Sales

WHILE IT MAY NOT BE CONVENTIONAL to start talking about business basics with sales, I believe it is the most important grounding you will need. Why? Well, you will choose your own path through this industry, as we discussed, through unpacking the available opportunities. But no matter what you do, you will be a salesperson. Going to be a grower? You are going to be selling your product and service to dispensaries. Going to be a dispensary owner? You are going to be selling to customers every day. Going to be an HVAC technician? You are going to be selling your services to growers. And so on ... you get the idea. Being a great salesperson is all about structuring an authentic conversation, understanding people, and getting them to reveal themselves and their needs to you.

We all have walls around us that no one can see, and they are especially strong when we feel uncomfortable. We put up our guard. Instances like this happen all the time: when we are sitting with a salesperson, when we go to a car lot, when we enter a store, when someone comes to the door we don't know, or when someone we don't know approaches us on the street. We aren't sure what to expect from the person, or we think the person may not have our best interests at heart, and so we put up our guard and we add a few more blocks to the invisible wall. If you, in your interactions, are someone who causes people to add more blocks to their walls, it is harder for you to get through to them. Even more troubling, in almost all cases, is that the person won't just say to you, "Hey, what you just said bothered me (hurt my feelings, irritated me, was not true), and this meeting is now over. Please leave." Instead, what will happen is that you (being unaware of yourself) will keep on going (chasing) and they will keep on avoiding (running), wasting everyone's time. Most important, you will never achieve the positive result you seek. That is sales, in a nutshell, for many people: the salesperson ineffectively chasing, and the customer running. That won't ever be you, after you read this.

Selling might be the most important skill that anyone has, and it is also the most completely misunderstood. There are more negative associations with salespeople than with most other professionals, and many of them are deserved because so few salespeople approach sales the right way. These associations are magnified because most of us are more likely to talk about the bad experiences we have over the great ones – especially sales experiences.

Here is what most people think sales is: the used car salesman, the late-night infomercial guy, talking people into things, always closing, smooth-talking, being slick, sharing shades of the truth, misleading people, and – at its worst – outright lying and dishonesty. That is not sales, and it's not professional. People who sell like this give the true professional salespeople a bad rap.

Here's what sales really is – or at least what it can be at its best: a structured, systematic, open, and honest conversation by equals, resulting in a continuation of the conversation if you both assess that there is a fit, or an ending of the conversation if there isn't (at least on that topic). Not every customer is a fit for what you offer, and you are not the right salesperson for everyone you encounter. It's not the end of the world. It really means you have just saved a tremendous amount of time, energy, and the emotional pain of having to "chase" people down and practically beg them to respond to you. That doesn't feel good to you, and it never feels good to the customer, either. There is a balance that a salesperson must strike between persistence and foolishness. Finding that balance depends on your ability to unpack what you can about the person in front of you.

If you remember, Mr. Spock from Star Trek stood way out from everyone else in the show because he famously prioritized logic over emotion, which is the opposite of how people are.

Emotions drive people more than intellect. Emotions move people, and logic follows. Consider that Bugatti sells a car for over a million dollars. Enough said. That's not a logical decision; it's an emotional one. Very likely, however, the emotional driver is this: "I want to be recognized in the world as being smart, successful, and rich." The buyers make an emotional decision, and *then* rationalize it with things that make it seem like logical thought: "I have the money and it could be a good investment." Examples like this exist all around us, from super boring purchases to big fancy ones. All those displays right by the registers are there because stores know that people will "impulse purchase" things as they are checking out. They didn't go into the store because they needed those items, but they'll walk out with them.

Given that emotions drive people – and therefore people's decisions during a sales transaction – it is critical that you learn to make your customers feel emotionally safe. Thomas Harris wrote a book entitled *I'm OK – You're OK*. The general idea of the book is that an analysis of transactions of all kinds reveals three observable ego-states: the Parent, the Adult, and the Child. His theory is that we're acting out of one of those three states at all times. When anyone feels, "I'm *not* okay," it can fuel people's feelings of vulnerability and lead to inappropriate emotional reactions of "the Child" that trigger the desire to evade. Simply put, we each have an "okay-ness" meter. When someone makes us feel "not okay," we will find a way to get rid of them. Conversely, when someone makes us feel "okay," we will want to be around them.

I remember I ran into a guy at a concert who I had worked with years earlier. As we were catching up in line at the bar, I mentioned that I had been through a difficult breakup, and was really down about it (heartbroken really, but I didn't totally divulge the level of pain). He said quickly, "Oh, you were probably just a rebound for her." I was so fuckin' mad in the moment because it hurt. It was as if he had said, "You weren't even there with her. None of it really mattered." I bullshitted with him through the night, but I haven't spoken to him since. Now, he could have said, "Wow, I feel for you man. We've all been there." That would have connected us, and brought us closer as human beings, but instead, what he said made me build a bigger wall. Now, he may have been trying to be honest, or felt like he was just being real with me, but whatever his reason, his comment made me shut him out. Unfortunately – and this is typical of most of us, particularly when we don't have a previous relationship to rely on – I didn't tell him he had hurt me because that would have felt like continuing to open myself up to being hurt. He might have made fun of me for being overly sensitive or just doubled down on the tough love and pushed me to see things his way.

In a sales situation, as mentioned before, your customers likely won't do you the service of telling you that you've made them build a wall; they'll just build it and move on. Ensuring that your customer feels "okay" with you is essential to the sales process. You must create a neutral space between you and the person you are talking to. If someone is neutral (at the least), they are open; if they are open, they can hear you; and if they can hear you, they can make a thoughtful choice. *That* is what you want to provide them: a choice to move forward or the freedom to say no. For example, my son's grandfather has a wonderful way to get children to try new foods. It's amazing. He says, "Try this, and if you don't like it, you can spit it out in my hand." Now, on some basic level, a child knows that it is an extreme solution to not liking a food item. But what that statement does is create a fairly neutral position to see if the child likes it or not. It's persuasive in getting the child to try it, encourages one to like it, but gives some power if they don't. Simple, right?

The way to do this in a sales situation is this: give someone a clear out. This is what you might say:

> *"By the end of this conversation, we are going to decide between two things. We are either going to continue this*

conversation because there is enough of a fit to keep going, or we will know this is not a fit and we can part as friends. If you know this is not a fit, will you please just tell me, 'No, this is not a fit for me'? (Secret weapon: people don't like to use the actual word no to other people. What they will do instead is tell you the truth about why it isn't a fit for them, and there shines the gold that will lead you into a deeper conversation.) If you do, I will just ask one question because I care about what I do and strive to do a good job. I would like to know why. Fair enough? If I don't feel this is a fit, I will tell you, and I'll tell you why. Okay?"

When you say this, and you really mean it, it creates neutrality.

I'm going to lay out a sales system for you, step by step, that ensures you create a neutral, emotionally safe place from which your customers can engage productively, and that enables you to take full and informed advantage of that engagement in the hopes of a productive interaction.

Here are the elements of the system in the order you will execute them:

- Research (if applicable)
- Connection
- Ground Rules
- Discovery (pain and motivation)
- Objections
- Budget
- Presentation
- Completion

RESEARCH

Be prepared for any meetings or interactions you have with potential customers. Your job is to be of service, and the foundation for that is to be prepared. The internet makes the world so much smaller in so many ways, not to mention resources like this book, so there is no excuse for being uninformed. If you are going to a meeting with a business owner, be sure you research everything you can about his or her business, and what the person may be good or bad at or struggling with at the moment. Research the field the business is in – what is happening in the market for all similar businesses that you might be a part of solving or enhancing? Research their main competitor, and be ready to talk about how you might offer a competitive edge. People feel seen and valued when you've done your homework. If your customer is more of an individual consumer, make sure you've researched their potential needs or questions. In a dispensary, this includes knowing everything you possibly can about what customers can use your product for, what challenges they may be facing that your product can help to solve, and all the ins and outs of your product and its uses. If you are providing a service (HVAC, plumbing, electricity, real estate), you better have researched exactly how your services apply for your customers, and be ready to answer questions they may have about how you provide your services.

CONNECTION

This is the part where you make sure your customer feels "okay." Too often, people like to jump right into the business at hand, but many important things can be learned by getting to know the person you are meeting or talking with. Usually, that information is more important than all the rest because it can help you understand what drives the person most. If you are meeting at an office, look around and see what is important to them (family pictures all over the office, sports paraphernalia, pictures of great historical figures, inspirational quotes, etc.). If you are meeting people in person, observe what they are wearing (their style, jewelry, work uniform, etc.), who they have with them, and any small details that may help you understand them. In all cases, pay attention to facial expressions and body language to help guide your assessment of what they are feeling and what state of mind they may be in. Then, use what information you have gathered to try and make an early connection with them. Get them to take down their invisible walls.

Examples:

- Grower to dispensary owner – "I love that picture of your family. I also have kids. They're the best, aren't they? How old are your kids now?"

    If the person warms to the conversation, you might make a connection to your why. "You know, I actually started growing after my second daughter was born because I realized I needed to pursue an opportunity that would help me save enough to send her to college. It might sound cheesy, but each time I walk into my grow room, I feel like I'm growing more than just plants, you know?" This might make him more interested in doing business with you if you both share a purpose. Only make this kind of connection if it's real and true. We can all sense bullshit from people.

1. Dispensary owner to customer – "Hello sir, I see that you're using a cane to get around right now. Can I possibly offer you a chair while we talk about what product I can offer you today? Everything we do here is about lessening your pain, so I'm at your service if I can make you more comfortable in any way."

2. Electrician to grower – "Hey, thanks so much for seeing me. It looks like you have a ton going on today. Are you guys just finishing up a cycle? (*Answer.*) Man, I admire you. I really think of myself as a specialist, and I like being able to focus in on just my particular craft, so I have no idea how you handle all the inputs and outputs of growing – from getting the right quality strains to finding the right employees, and managing a pristine grow room through each phase of the plant ... it's a lot!" (*This is an opportunity to make him feel seen, but also to show that you know about his business.*)

GROUND RULES

If you follow baseball at all, you may already know that every baseball park in the US and Canada is slightly different from each other. Some have higher walls than others, some have half walls, some have the walls closer in ... and one has a big green monster. The umpires and the managers from each team get together BEFORE the game starts in each stadium to discuss the rules and agree on them. For example, if the ball hits the yellow line on the top of the wall, then it is determined at that time if it is an infield double, and if it rolls over the wall, then it is a home run. The main point is that if they tried to hold that "discussion" during the game, there would be utter chaos, and undoubtedly people would feel like decisions were being made that favored one team over another. Making the rules up as you go along, or playing a game where not everyone knows the rules, never plays well or ends well.

This step is critical in the sales process because it sets up the entire interaction. During the ground rules portion of your interaction, you want to ask permission for things you think will be critical to assessing fit, and name anything you think might be important for both of you to agree on upfront (research will help you set the right ground rules). If you ask permission to discuss "whatever needs to be discussed" to come to a conclusion at the end of this conversation, you now have permission from that person to ask almost anything (anything that would still maintain their okayness). If that person breaks the rules, you can gently refer back to the previously agreed-upon ground rules.

Examples:

In a meeting –

You: Stephen, would it be out of the question for us to set up some ground rules for this meeting?

Stephen: Um, sure.

You: Good, thanks. I want to make sure we create a space where we can be comfortable asking each other the necessary questions to see if this is a fit.

Stephen: Makes sense.

You: I only have two in mind: One, I just want to ask that we give each other permission to interrupt this conversation any time we need clarification to better understand the other person. And two, I'd love for us to commit to being open, honest, and quite frankly, even vulnerable about what matters to determine if there is a fit for us both. If you really don't think this is right for you, will you tell me?

Stephen (likely): Sure.

You: Great, thank you.

In a store –

Have you ever had a conversation with someone who keeps answering the phone? It's totally rude, in my opinion, but what can you say in the moment – "hang up"? You have no agreement with the person regarding phone use, but you disagree (clearly) that it's appropriate. One way you can set ground rules with your customers in the store is to post a friendly and welcoming sign at the entrance that lists your "Rules of Service." It might read:

- *Let's leave phones out of this. We want to focus on your every need, and we want to be sure you tell us everything we can do for you.*

- *We all keep voice levels low here out of respect for our customers who have come to us feeling unwell. Thanks for helping us to be a caring community!*

It's not perfect, and likely customers will break a rule. However, if that happens, you have the ability to politely ask them to make a shift, given what you're trying to accomplish. If they won't, then you don't actually want their business because their decisions are affecting other customers.

Like the professionals who work together in baseball parks, we all feel better when we know the rules going into the game. It makes people feel calm and able to engage effectively. When it's applicable, don't forget to ask them if they have any ground rules they want to set up before engaging. This gives them power in the conversation and makes them more likely to be open.

The last thing and for some, possibly the toughest thing, is if someone will not agree to ground rules for a meeting. I cancel it. You have to. This is a fair meeting between two adults, and if someone will not consent to this basic agreement, then there is either a deeper problem or they don't respect you as an equal. It's a red flag. Hold your ground and stand strong for yourself, your future, and your family.

DISCOVERY

In a world of no concrete answers, questions are the answer. Questions do two amazing things for salespeople. First, while someone is answering a question, they are not focusing on you, but on their thoughts and their answer. That is important in sales because if they're doing this, then they aren't comparing you to all the other shitty salespeople they have encountered before and discounting you before you can get started. Second, and most important, when other people are talking, you are learning. Your job as a salesperson is to learn first, then talk.

During discovery, one thing you are trying to uncover is the person's, or company's, current pain and desired gain. Pain, as we discussed earlier in the book, is the real driver of so many things.

It has been proven that people will do more to eradicate pain than to get more gain. For example, psychologically, most people feel that *losing* $20 is worse than *not gaining* a new $20. Since pain is also a major driver of our emotions, and emotions drive our decisions, many people's decisions will be tied back to their pain. Very likely, the person's pain is the reason they are talking to you at all. They have probably expressed some sort of reason for wanting you there, so you need to make sure you've fully unpacked it so you know what you are trying to solve with your product or service. What is their intellectual reason to be there? What is their real issue? What is the underlying pain that is causing them to take action right now? What is their desired gain? What is their why?

There is a simple bridge that allows you to move into a conversation driven by questions that uncover pain. You can't just ask someone, "What's your pain?" because it would feel awkward, and sharing pain requires vulnerability that you haven't made safe yet. Therefore, you bridge into questions about pain by first helping the person see that they are not alone in the pain they are experiencing. You can do this by using the research you've done around the industry and this person's company to share with them some of the most common problems people in their situation face (you should be able to get close to what their pain might be). For example, when I was a sales trainer, and meeting with sales managers and C-level leaders to offer them my services, here's how I would launch my discovery:

Me: Vince, can I tell you the top three things we've helped people with in sales?

Vince: Of course.

Me: One, leaders find that their salespeople are on a roller-coaster – two months they're off-the-charts great, and then the next three months they're below average. Two, on a ten-person sales team, four people do the majority of the numbers. Three, some people you hire were great interviewees, but don't end up working out as employees long term *(throughout this, read Vince's face to look for agreement or understanding)*. Have you experienced any of these issues, OR am I way off base?

Ideally, Vince resonates with one or more of the three problems I named, because through my research I believe I am going to be close with one of these things, and I know they are common industry problems. However, if Vince's pain doesn't reside in one of these, I have at least proven that I have strong industry knowledge, and reminded him that leaders throughout the industry *have* pain, even if it's not the same as his. If one of the three I named land, I can now dive into questions about it to discover more specificity around his pain, and he will be open to sharing. If he says that his problem lies elsewhere, I have invited him to start telling me about it, and my questioning can follow from that.

Here are probing questions you can use to uncover pain:

BUSINESSES	INDIVIDUAL CONSUMERS
• What is the motivation for you to talk right now? • How long have you been dealing with the issue? • What is the financial cost? • What is the emotional cost? • What have you tried to fix it? • What keeps you up at night? • If my service/product helped you, what would the ideal result be?	• What brings you in today? • How long have you been dealing with this? • Do you mind sharing a bit about the physical toll this has taken so I understand your need better? • Can I ask you a personal question? (Yes.) How are you holding up emotionally? • What have you already tried? • What have your doctors recommended? • Which of your symptoms is the most troubling for you? • Is there anything that makes you feel nervous about using marijuana products? *In a dispensary, you could ask customers to fill out a questionnaire to get these answers so that they don't have to talk out loud about things that are personal. Then your salespeople can quickly read them before helping to find the right product.* *Consider a store "ground rule" that says you will always ask questions of your customers because you want to know their pains/desires.*

OBJECTIONS

Objections are important because most people completely misunderstand what is really happening when someone offers one. It typically goes like this:

- Customer: I think the price is too high.

- Salesperson: (taking the bait) Let me see if I can reduce it. (Or some version of that.)

Typical objections:
- The price seems too high.
- I don't have the money.
- I need to think about it.
- I don't have time to make a decision right now.
- I need more information.
- I'm not interested.

Here is how you handle any and every objection with just one question: "I'm not sure what you mean by that. Would you mind explaining it to me in a bit more detail?" Dig deeper on whatever a potential customer says because you really don't know exactly what's going on, and you shouldn't assume you do. Plus, sometimes, believe it or not, a potential customer may make up an objection to get out of an uncomfortable situation. Asking a question also flushes out more information, which is what you need to provide a solution.

Here is the dance of salesperson and customer:

> *Customer*: Doesn't want to make a mistake, a bad decision, or look foolish, because they have been burned before or have buyer's remorse. May fear the unknown or the loss of self-esteem as a result of the wrong choice.

> *Salesperson*: Wants to be powerful, know everything about the product/service, look smart, have all the answers, and be the one who makes the difference.

You can see that, if this is true, the customer will have a difficult time being vulnerable and revealing their true needs and feelings. Their walls will be up to protect themselves. And you, wanting to be a polished, smart, and informed salesperson, will have a hard time asking questions because it may make you look weak. But your job as the salesperson is to take bricks out of the customer's wall, not add more to it. People are a mystery. It doesn't matter how *you* feel about things or what *you* would do. It matters how *they* feel and what *they* want to do.

BUDGET

This is a topic most salespeople like to avoid. Salespeople usually like to talk about their own prices, specials, and deals, but not what the customer's real budget is. However, if you can understand the customer's budget upfront before you present your own prices, you've won a huge battle. When you know the budget, you can align your sale directly to it (or end the sale if you realize it's impractical). Interestingly, most people will tell you if you just ask them. If anyone squabbles or avoids sharing, you can always refer back to the agreement you made in the beginning (ground rules) to ask the questions that need to be asked in order to understand if you are a fit or not. Boom.

Example:

"Eric, would you be willing to share your budget with me, in rough numbers? I won't hold you to it; I just need an idea. When you purchased things similar to this, how did you evaluate the potential costs?"

For a business transaction, more so than in an individual customer sale, you also want to try and understand how the person will make the choice to do business with you or not. Ask them how they evaluate the factors involved to make a choice that is right for them. You need to know, for example, before you present your solution to their pain, if all the people who need to be there in order for the decision to be made, are present. You also need to know what the time frame is for making the decision. Don't present anything if the circumstances for a decision don't align.

Example:

You: Candace, how will you choose what is best for you regarding this decision?

Candace: My partner and I will need to talk through numbers and make a decision together.

You: Okay, great. Any chance they are around so I can share this same information them too? If not, is there a time I can come back to catch both of you together?

Ultimately, you want to be the one making the pitch to the decision-makers, and/or the people in charge of the budget, so be sure you're talking to all of them.

PRESENTATION

This is your moment to shine, or your moment to excuse yourself from the conversation. If you've followed the process, listened to the answers, and stayed strong in the meeting, you already know if you can help this person or if you can't.

If you know you can, align all of the information you have gathered through this process and present to those facts: the needs you know you can meet, the problem you can solve, and the almighty pain you can eliminate to set them free. This should be the easiest part because they have done all the work for you by sharing the answers you need in order to make a case to them. You can blow their minds with this presentation because it's customized specifically to them. It's like having all the answers to a test. Importantly, this type of presentation also totally honors the person and their time. You are pitching them on what they want and need, not what *you* want them to want and need. This is true for a business person running a business, and for a customer looking for a product in your shop.

A few examples of aligned language:

"You said that quality is a very important consideration for you. According to WeedMaps (which is a rating service for marijuana stores), we have a five-star rating."

"You mentioned having a consistent product every time is something that keeps you up at night. We use the same plants to create the same strains, and test every batch before we release it for sale."

COMPLETION

Sometimes people can have second thoughts, buyer's remorse, or something can come up. So, when you complete this process, you need to probe a little more to make sure they are comfortable with their decision and uncover any additional potential problems.

Example:

"Nancy, you said that you wanted to discuss this decision with your husband, and we are going to talk this Friday. Is there anything you anticipate he might say that would change your mind?" (*This gives you a chance to give her an argument for those issues before she encounters them.*)

Additionally, sometimes people make decisions and then don't make themselves available for follow-through. Make sure you set some ground rules for communication.

Example:

"Nancy, when I call on Friday, what should I do if you are not available? If I leave a message and I don't hear back from you, what do you want me to do?"

Here you are pressing a bit, obviously, but you are signaling to this person that you are going to follow through and complete this process.

If you research, connect, set ground rules, discover pain, assess budget, present alignment, and complete the process, you will successfully engage in every sales opportunity, and both you and your customer will leave believing your time and interests have been respected.

IT'S NO GAME

DAVID BOWIE

Competition

COMPETITION IN BUSINESS IS NO GAME. You want to understand where you fit in the market and how you will differentiate yourself from others. As we discussed, this is a critical part of creating your business plan, but dealing with competition takes upkeep through a vigilant awareness of industry trends, market shifts, new entries in the market, and current competitor changes. This ongoing awareness, partnered with a business plan that prepares you to flex as needed, will be a recipe for success. I like to think about addressing competition in five ways:

- Know how you are unique.

- Know your context and competition.

- Stay grounded in excellent and sustaining systems.

- Value your people.

- Stay ahead.

The first two are about how you set up and run your business; the third is the absolutely critical way to keep market share and profit in a busy industry; the last two are about maintaining your edge, as customer loyalty can sustain you through a lot of unpredictable market changes.

KNOW HOW YOU ARE UNIQUE

As you work on this part of your business plan, consider the following questions:

- What are the benefits you offer customers?

- Do you have better quality than competitors? Better service?

- Do you specialize in any particular products or needs?

- Is your store environment a draw?

- Why would someone ultimately want to come back to your store after their first visit?

- How do you use convenient technology to help customers?

- How do you see the future of the industry, and how are you positioned to guide your customers through changes?

In a perfect world, you could say that you do ALL of these better than your competitors, but make sure that's true if you're going to advertise that way. I recommend thinking through the strengths of yourself and your business plan, and aligning your marketed unique traits to where you are the strongest. These are the areas you will be most likely to maintain. And remember – don't engage in the rat trap of dropping prices … it's a deadly race to the bottom.

KNOW YOUR CONTEXT AND COMPETITION

During the time I recently mentioned when I was running a retail business with a good friend, I was so naive and knew so little. When my friend and I were just starting out with our business, I got shopped. Getting shopped, for those of you who don't know, means that a competitor comes into your store to check you out, grill you, and try to get you to talk as much as possible while acting like they're a customer. The main purpose is to uncover the advantages or disadvantages of the competition and then use that information to kick the shit out of you with current and potential customers (in the nicest way possible, of course).

We were considered a "mom and pop" operation, and our main competitor (who shopped me) had four locations and a large warehouse (they were "mom and pop" too, but bigger and more established than we were). As I was talking to the guy shopping me, I said something like, "We have a lean operation here to keep costs down and focus our attention on you." I found out later that after he learned this from me, when a customer came into his store, he would say, "Hey, have you been down the street to those other guys (implying he has nothing to be afraid of)? Nice guys, but I'm worried their operation is a little lean, and if nothing goes wrong, you may be all right, but this is a major purchase for you. I'm guessing you want a company that has the resources and facilities to handle anything that comes up." It was subtle but smooth. I was so proud of our store, and so young, that I probably talked to that guy for an hour. Now I know not to offer that kind of information, of course, so I hope you can learn from my early mistakes. The funny part of this whole story is that I eventually became good friends with the guy.

Here are a few old-school and new-school ways to get to know your competition better:

Old-school method (OSM): Shop them, obviously. Nothing like an actual retail experience to get a feel for another person's business, and as I am an example, people will often tell you more than you'd expect.

New-school method (NSM): Look at their websites and glean what you can. There is a ton of information there.

OSM: Drive the neighborhood where you want to put your location, or where you are already located, and note the competition, marketing, visibility, and anything else you can find to get a picture of your immediate area.

NSM: Use the maps feature on your phone and find out how many locations are within ten miles, then use Google Earth to put in addresses and look at storefronts and surrounding areas.

OSM: Compile information about each competitor in a file that you can add to (leaflets, printed reviews, etc.).

NSM: Look at their job postings and see what they are currently saying about themselves.

OSM: Try to uncover their unique capability (if they have one) and likely next move in the market (edibles, makeup, etc.).

NSM: See if you can find and follow them through social media that customers use, to get a sense of how they are positioning themselves with people.

There are a lot of approaches to getting – and staying – familiar with your competition. Make sure you at least know the basics: their mission/vision statement, their competitive advantage, their story, what they sell, how much it costs, who owns it, who they are (biography), how many years they have been in the business, and what customers they target.

STAY GROUNDED IN EXCELLENT AND SUSTAINING SYSTEMS

This is a critical part of this book and your success: there are many marijuana businesses right now that do not have strong business fundamentals and are getting by successfully because the demand for the product is so high. When this market opens up to real competition, meaning business people who are currently on the sidelines because of the federal restrictions, the businesses with strong growing systems and strong fundamentals will win the long-term battle for market share.

Here's a comparison to help you think about the difference between an organization living on its "product" instead of its practice. In 2018, the Pittsburgh Steelers had the most talent in the NFL, everyone knew that and it was confirmed by their eight Pro Bowl selections. Pro Bowl selections are made by coaches, players, and fans. Each group votes equally as one-third of the decision. However, despite having incredible individual talent, the Steelers are loose, emotional, personality-based, and they lose games – especially big games – because of it. When pressure is at its greatest, character and systems matter more.

In comparison, the New England Patriots had four players selected in 2018 (half of what the Steelers had), yet they have a dominating record against most teams, particularly the Steelers. Currently, Tom Brady is 11–2 in his career against the Steelers. That is the highest mark of any starting quarterback against any single team since 1991. How does this happen? The Patriots take older project players and "cast off" players (ones that don't play well on other teams) and get the best out of them. They dominate the Steelers with mostly inferior talent, except at quarterback, because they have a training and execution system that consistently gets more out of their people.

As you start your business in this industry, one of the most critical edges you can give yourself over the competition is an organization that can sustain excellence over time.

VALUE YOUR PEOPLE

The other major edge you can maintain over your competition is developing strong loyalty in the two main cohorts that impact your business: your employees and your customers. In the next section (Get Educated: The Business – People), we will talk more in-depth about how to value your employees, so here we will focus on valuing your customers and why that is such a major factor in addressing the competition.

Here's the deal: while my grow system will result in an incredibly high-quality product, and there is a lot of variation in marijuana quality, this industry is still somewhat a commodity business. A commodity is defined as "an interchangeable product."

Meaning, a product that is basically identical to another. Most customers don't actually know the difference between products unless someone in the store can explain it to them, but once they have experienced a product they like, they want and expect that same thing every time. If they can get that same product in other places, you need to be sure that the experience they have getting it from you ensures that they associate the buying experience *with* that product they want. So let's take a look at another "commodity" industry and think about how it should guide our focus on valuing customers.

I was watching a game in the Pepsi Center, one of the main stadiums in Colorado, and was astonished that the entire building was built around a company that essentially sells sugar water that isn't even good for you. It got me thinking about cola as an industry. Off the top of my head, I thought about each of these and described them to myself.

COKE:	**PEPSI:**
Brown-colored soda	*Brown-colored soda*
Sugar drink	*Sugar drink*
Sweet tasting	*Sweet tasting*
Burns your throat a little	*Burns your throat a little*
if you drink it fast	*if you drink it fast*
Tastes a little different	*Tastes a little different*
from Pepsi	*from Coke*

They seemed so similar that when I got home, I looked up each to see what they actually were. Here is the list of official ingredients named in each:

FROM COKE:

Carbonated water

High-fructose corn syrup

Caramel color

Phosphoric acid

Natural flavors

Caffeine

FROM PEPSI:

Carbonated water

High-fructose corn syrup

Caramel color

Sugar

Phosphoric acid

Citric acid

Natural flavors

Caffeine

Are these not nearly identical, or what? How long has there been the Coke vs. Pepsi war? Coke and Pepsi are commodities *and simultaneously* loyalty products. Loyalty products are those whose sales are driven by customer preference for a specific brand of a product (regardless of any similarities it may have to others). So how do they battle it out for customers if their product is so similar? Each maintains unique "relationships" with their customers, breeding that customer loyalty. Most people have a distinct preference for one or the other, and they stick to it. Coke and Pepsi advertise differently to customers to appeal to people and draw them in. These two massive companies know the value of their customers.

Coke and Pepsi are, strikingly, similar to the cannabis industry. If you want to start a dispensary or marijuana-related business, it will inevitably share a lot of similarities with other companies like it: you are growing a plant that can be reproduced by others. You can and should distinguish yourself in ways that complement your strengths, but you better believe that one of your most important assets is your customer loyalty. Taking care of customers will mean returning business and referrals. You want to become a part of people's routine, the rhythm that makes them feel centered and safe. The work we've done around knowing yourself can be translated to knowing your customers and building lasting relationships with them. They need to believe that you truly care about them and their needs … and it must be true. This is the most important differentiator for you.

Imagine you are an electrician wanting to specialize in the marijuana industry. Each electrician builds their knowledge base over time, but ultimately electrical services are commodities – at least in the eyes of those who are seeking services. You want to create an electrical company that breeds customer loyalty through the relationships you build that drive a desire for your "brand."

Here is something to think about: How many times have you heard:

- Our customer service is number one.
- Our people make the difference.
- We have the lowest prices.
- We have the best service.
- We care about you.
- Satisfaction guaranteed.
- Nobody beats our deals.

Doesn't it seem like every company is basically saying the same thing? I mean, what company says, "Nine times out of ten we're great. It's that one time that messes us up every time." People spend a lot of time trying to distract you from what they aren't good at by naming their strengths, and not enough time working to make sure they handle mistakes well. Honestly, I'd like to hear this latter slogan from someone because it's not whether you make mistakes or piss people off. You will. It's how you respond to a mistake that counts. Don't focus your time on thinking about what you'll say about your business to bring in customers; focus your time on what you are actually doing for customers. And when you don't get it right the first time, make it right as soon as you can.

The point is this: differentiating comes down to the customer experience. The goal we are shooting for is having a quality, consistent, and recognizable product, AND an experience that is worth paying more for.

STAY AHEAD

Is it just me, or is anyone else blown away that the ride-sharing companies are the largest businesses in the taxi space, and all they did was come up with a software program? Those companies, like Uber and Lyft, don't own anything: not cars, or maintenance facilities, or training centers, or anything else – and yet they have supplanted traditional taxi services in a matter of a few years.

Things will disrupt the marijuana industry. Questions to consider:

- What technologies could change things almost overnight? How am I staying updated on trends and new ideas?

- Could new vendors eventually compete with me by changing customer expectations (marijuana delivery, online ordering ...)?

- Who could expand in or enter this market and disrupt it?

- How can I stay on top of these things and incorporate them into my strategy?

Figure out what publications to read, sites to follow, conferences to attend, and people to know, and make it your business to stay ahead of trends and movement in this industry. Your competition likely won't.

PAID IN FULL

ERIC B. & RAKIM

Pricing

THE TRAP IN PRICING IS THAT SOME COMPANIES will try to price every-one out of business by creating a race to the bottom. Look at fast food: everyone has dollar menus now. They have all cut their own profits, but to stay alive as a business, you can't compete in a race to the bottom in pricing unless you're also finding a way to reduce expenses dramatically. Otherwise, you're just diminishing your returns in a game that's very hard to win ... and winning still leaves you with a narrower profit margin than you used to have.

The greatest example of this is an early "competitor" to U-Haul. I put competitor in quotes because of a major flaw in their business model for gaining market share that blew up in their face, undermining their attempt to compete. The Jartran story is interesting because of how it started. You've likely heard of Ryder trucks. Mr. Ryder started Ryder Truck Leasing. The company now has over $5 billion in revenue and operates in many countries, but it started with a $30 down payment on a Model A truck in 1933. The company did incredibly well over time, but in 1978, Mr. Ryder was being pushed out of control of Ryder Truck Leasing, and eventually left the company he founded, in anger. He decided to start a competitor to Ryder, and he used his initials and chopped the word transportation to create "Jartran." Big mistake. It cost him his fortune of nearly $100 million (in today's money). The fundamental flaw in his plan was his pricing.

Here's the deal: if you own a truck outright, and it cost you $30,000, you have invested $30,000 plus upkeep fees, ongoing insurance, and licensing costs. If you rented that truck for $200 a day, it would only take 150 days to get that $30,000 back to you. That would leave you 215 days of the year to make a profit. Let's say you only rent it out for half of those days (107.5). That would still result in a profit of $21,500, minus repairs and insurance. Not bad.

U-Haul, the other major player in the truck rental market, owned its trucks (reflecting the model I just described), and Jartran leased its trucks. When you lease trucks, you have to pay for the truck, even if it's sitting there not being rented. Once you deduct the payment for the truck, upkeep fees, insurance, and repairs, there isn't much profit left. The only way to continue with the business is to fund it from your pocket. Foolish. To further complicate this, Jartran purposely undercut the competition and a reasonable fee with its pricing to gain market share. They priced their rental trucks for $100 a day, forcing U-Haul to lower its prices and lose both money and valuable expansion.

The net result: Jartran went bankrupt and U-Haul won the war, but it cost U-Haul a whopping $500,000,000 in profit and more in debt. All of this likely stemmed from the disrespect and hurt feelings of Ryder, and his reckless attempt to get back at Ryder for taking over what he had built. He was focused on capturing the market and didn't think through the long game.

As we recently discussed, you should be planning for both an ambitious and a conservative result as you prepare to launch your business. One place in your plan where thinking through both eventualities will be important is in your financial forecasting (see more details in the next chapter). Pricing is a part of this. It's true that you may need to adjust pricing over time to ensure that you are a reasonable player in the market, and you want to know in advance about how much wiggle room up and down that your financial model can withstand (in comparison to your expenses). You just don't want to rely on lowering pricing as the main way to compete – it's not sustainable, nor is it unique to you. Anyone can lower prices.

You will need to research medical and recreational dispensaries in the area where you choose to assess pricing, but here is a *very* basic set of guidelines for marijuana weights (all dependent on strain, quality, and the form you are selling it in):

You need to have pricing for these weights: Gram, Eighth, Quarter, Half, and Ounce. I was going to offer suggested pricing, but they change quickly and regionally, so consult with us to help you if needed.

Ultimately, you need to get the pricing right, but don't depend on pricing to solve any problems for you. Your hook with customers will be the care you give them.

MARKETING

TUA

Marketing (Obviously

PART OF DEVELOPING THAT HOOK WITH CUSTOMERS (and beating competitors) is having a strong marketing strategy in your business plan. Marketing has been defined as "putting the right product in the right place, at the right price, at the right time." In order to accomplish this, you must think carefully through several important facets of your business. The classic marketing facets are known as the three Cs of marketing:

- Customer
- Company
- Competitor

The idea is that these three facets should be at the center of your marketing strategy and that they should be approached independently, but cross-checked to ensure they align and complement each other. This type of approach has come to be known as the marketing mix. It ensures you are tackling all the elements of marketing, with the right "mix of ingredients" to get what you want.

Another common set of marketing facets is the four Ps:

- Price
  - Price to Customer Cost

- Product
  - Product to Customer Solution

- Place
  - Place to Customer Convenience

- Promotion
  - Promotion to Customer Communication

The sub-bullets are reminders to keep the customer at the center of our planning, thereby ensuring we serve them to the best of our abilities. As we covered, customer retention and loyalty are your best levers against competition.[1]

As you can see, there is a lot to think about and plan for in marketing, and it is probably the most thought-about and talked-about concern of business owners and CEOs. It is the make-or-break part of your business, because even if you have the greatest product imaginable and it will change the world, but no one knows about it – you're sunk.

---

[1] *https://www.cleverism.com/understanding-marketing-mix-concept-4ps/*

In a nutshell:

- A business plan sells the company and makes sure it can accomplish its purpose.

- A marketing plan lays out how you plan to sell the products/services offered by the company.

In an industry growing as fast as this one, perhaps the most important step in building your marketing plan is truly knowing your intended market. The plan is to get a clear picture of the customer base for your product: growth trends, overall size, competition, specific challenges, specific needs, and any other trends you can gather from researching the market you plan to sell to. You'll want to have a fact-based approach here. In order to do this type of market research, you need to define your ideal customer (and/or expected customer): age range, gender, education level, profession(s), marital status, income level, location, lifestyle, reason for marijuana need/desire, and other needs. This shouldn't limit you, but it will help you get clear on how you set up your product offerings and customer service, as well as how and where you appeal to your audience. You can also survey your customers as you get to know them and start to seek trends in their responses that let you adapt ongoing products, services, and marketing strategies to the customer base that's showing up. At the end of your market research, challenge yourself to write an answer to the question, "What do my customers care about most, and how am I meeting them in that space?"

BALL OF CONFUSION
(THAT'S WHAT THE WORLD IS TODAY)

THE TEMPTATIONS

Online Marketing

ISN'T IT INTERESTING THAT WE HAVE MANY MORE ways to communicate than ever, yet studies suggest that our relationships are not as strong? As technology continues to change so quickly, some of us find ourselves confused; however, we need to embrace these tools because they can make a huge difference in success and our image. It's foolish not to utilize your website, social media, and video.

Many companies offer website templates you can plug into for a monthly fee. I hired someone because I wanted a different look entirely, and besides your employees and physical location, it is the most prominent customer-facing part of your business. You know that people will evaluate how successful your business is, and how reliable (modern, friendly, fun, etc.) your company is, based on your website. So here are important things to consider when hiring a web designer:

- Who owns the intellectual property?
  a. Is your designer performing work under the copyright act?
  b. Make sure the developer will not infringe on copyright or others' intellectual property.

- Is all content on the site (graphics, domain, code, software, and programming) solely owned by you?

- Who is responsible for securing various licenses, clearances, and copyrighted material rights, if needed?

- Does the developer's other work (be sure you see some) meet your standards? Do they have a specific style that aligns with your vision?

- Can the developer give you references from past work? What do those references say about the developer's quality of work, timeliness, and ability to translate vision into unique web design (does he/she listen well)?

- Are they willing to help you think through the connections between your website and social media sites (Facebook, LinkedIn, Instagram, Twitter)?

Online touchpoints for your business, whether your website or other social media, will also become a place for people to communicate about your business. Given all the work you'll be doing to set it up successfully, hopefully a lot of what you hear is positive. However, it may also be a place where people go to criticize you if they did not enjoy their experience or product. In the old days, someone would have to face a business owner person-to-person in order to have a complaint heard. Now that people can voice their opinions relatively (or completely) anonymously, people feel a protected freedom to say whatever they want. They don't have to face you to do it.

Complaints are really just people's opinions about what they experienced, and they are most often a way to vent when frustrated. These days, if you want to share your "opinion," you just have to get online, drop a "review bomb" and sign off. These bombs usually don't help businesses get better because they can't follow up to get more information, and evidence shows that complaints like this aren't ultimately fulfilling for the person dropping them. These negative reviews may make someone feel better in the moment, but they often don't result in a resolution or change moving forward. Even if a business wanted to address and remedy negative reviews, it's very hard to do when they are posted online.

So what can you do about this? How do you avoid having your online footprint stained by customer venting and dissatisfaction? As an owner of a business, one of the most important ways to serve your customers is to offer them the opportunity to let you know if their experience or product isn't what they hoped for. Don't assume that if you and your employees are friendly, people will be comfortable sharing complaints with you. You have to explicitly ask for that feedback as close to in-the-moment as possible. You can do this by having the last person to interact with the customer

GET EDUCATED — THE BUSINESS — THE BASICS

check in on their experience. You can send an immediate text within twenty-four hours after a sale to see if the product was to their liking. You can post signs and offer feedback cards for people to use in your store/business to give more opportunities for people to talk to you if they are upset. Here's an example of a sign you might post:

We Care ...
Our existence is based on serving you. We take it seriously, and we're easy to talk to. Having said that, we cannot read minds. If you ever have an unsatisfactory experience on any level, please tell us. We not only welcome the feedback but if you uncover a flaw in our operation, you will be rewarded.

The more of these opportunities you provide, the more likely it is that you will diffuse the "review bomb" before it gets dropped.

Next, you have to take the complaint seriously. Really listen to your customers and respond to them when you can. Tell them how you are going to fix whatever problem they experienced. As we will discuss, any type of feedback is valuable to you – absorb it and make the best of it. Will you always agree with the complaint? No. Will your customers always be right? No. However, whatever they share is an accurate reflection of their perspective and experience, so even if you are just healing their perception by being open and responsive, it's worth it.

I once went to a restaurant with a friend after hearing that they had incredible vegetarian tamales. My friend ordered the beef tamales, and I ordered the vegetarian ones. When they came, they looked identical. I told the waiter I thought they had made a mistake. He told me that the vegetarian tamales were made with a product that looked like beef. He could tell by the look on my face that I wasn't convinced. He told me he would get the manager for me. The manager came over and confirmed what the waiter had told me, but then he did something brilliant. He said, "You know what, sir? I really want you to be fully satisfied, so let me take these back and have them make you a fresh order of vegetarian tamales. I will personally make sure that you get the right ones."

When he brought the new order, there were identical to my first order. I had been wrong, and they had given me the correct order the first time. However, the manager was not addressing the correctness of my concern; he was addressing the confusion and uncertainty my concern had created for me, and making sure I felt good about my experience. Not only did I end up enjoying the food, but I left incredibly impressed with the restaurant and the manager. If this restaurant had not set up a system where every customer issue was addressed with sincere concern, I might have gone home and given them a low rating online. Instead, I actually found the manager before I left and apologized for making a mistake that created extra work. He assured me it had been no problem at all.

The best way to control your online footprint is to manage your customer service so that people don't need an online venue to be heard. Have faith that almost anything can be worked out when we are IN communication.

ALL THE PLACES

PETE ROCK & C.L. SMOOTH

Choosing Real Estate

AN IMPORTANT PART OF YOUR BUSINESS PLAN and your financing is figuring out what real estate you need to execute your plan. We'll cover things you should consider for commercial grows, as well as dispensary locations.

One of the first things you need to consider is if you are going to buy locations, or rent/lease them. The commercial grows I managed were in rental spaces and were connected through the dispensaries. I leased them with the full knowledge of the property owner. If you can buy a place, great. That is the best plan for the long run, and it gives you maximum control over your environment. Buying will also take a lot of capital, so leasing a place is a perfectly fine option as long as you are meticulous about going through the lease with a fine-toothed comb. I have a lot of experience in real estate, a real estate license, and I've leased many properties. Here are a few pitfalls to avoid and property requirements to consider.

LEASE PITFALLS TO AVOID

- Don't sign a lease without having your lawyer look it over.

- Always be sure you know if the lease has, or the criteria for, a landlord's right to terminate the lease early. Try to avoid leases that have this.

- Avoid any requirement of a personal guarantee on the lease.

- Avoid any disclaimer about any services provided to you.

- Make sure there is no allowance for the landlord to pass on increased operating costs to you.

- Look for language about escalating expenses over time.

PROPERTY REQUIREMENTS TO CONSIDER

For either a grow space or a dispensary space, think through these questions and make sure the answers you need align to the space you choose and any lease you sign (your lawyer can help you with this).

Use:
- What is the permitted use of the property?

- Does the landlord/owner condone your operation?

- Can you sublease the space?

- Are there any zoning rules that impact your business, given its nature?

Space:
- What is the usable square footage?

- What is the price per square foot?

- For grows, is there capacity to add electrical and HVAC as needed?

Lease Terms and Rates:
- What are the terms for length and price?

- Does the rate increase year after year?

- What are the late fees?

- Can the landlord terminate the lease early?

- What is the fee if you want to terminate the lease early?

Lease Options:
- Do you have the option to renew the lease?

- What is the duration of the option? When does it expire?

- Is there a lease option to purchase available?

Security Deposit:
- What is the amount?

- Can a letter of credit be used in lieu of it?

- When will the deposit be returned?

- What are the terms for getting the deposit back?

Tenant Improvements (this is an important one):
- What improvements will be needed? This is critical because the owner will own them. You need to be sure the ones you want to make are allowed and be clear about who owns any associated "hardware" from the improvements.

- Can you do the work yourself or choose your own contractor? If not, what are the quotes for the work?

- Given the answers to No. 2, how much time will it take to complete?

- Are any permits necessary?

- Will the owner contribute to the improvements?

- Will you be paying rent while the improvements are being done?

Repairs:
- What is your responsibility for repairs?

- Are there stipulations about how the cause of the repair impacts responsibility?

Act of God:
- If there is a hurricane, tornado, or flood, for example, what are your obligations?

- Is the lease canceled in that event?

- Do you collect any of the insurance money from such an event? Do you need to have separate insurance to cover such an event?

Utilities:
- Are they individually metered?

- For grows, does the landlord understand and condone what your electricity and HVAC needs will do to utility prices?

Security:
- Does the location have any built-in security?

- Given the location, what additional security would be needed?

Signage:
- What signs are permitted?

- Are there regulations regarding the exterior of the building?

Parking (mostly for dispensaries):
- How many spaces are allotted?

- Are there options for more?

- How is the lighting?

You've heard the famous saying about successful real estate, "Location, location, location." It is absolutely true – especially for a dispensary – and you can piggyback off a brilliant company that has already done all the research and work for you about how to choose a great location. Who would that company be? McDonald's. If you happened to see the movie *The Founder*, you know it is based on Ray Kroc, the 'founder' of McDonald's. An interesting element of the McDonald's story is that one of the largest levers of the company's success is actually its real estate empire.

Here are some factors that McDonald's considers for its locations: The ideal store location is on a corner. There are two places to put up signage on major streets. A site near an intersection with traffic lights is best. A site that has a lot of parking. A store that has the right population allowances. And finally, an ideal store size of 5,000 square feet.

Since McDonald's has done all this research for you, you can either look for a location like this or just find a location near a McDonald's. The plus side of this second option is that people have actually taken the time to prove that McDonald's is popular with cannabis users. A *Forbes* article by Debra Borchardt stated, "The online survey, which had 27,500 respondents, was conducted in twenty-five markets where marijuana has been legalized, with a base population of 55 million. Some 8.5 percent of the survey respondents purchased cannabis from a legally authorized dispensary. In the past four weeks, 43 percent of those marijuana customers said they ate at McDonald's." It's a win-win.

If you decide to purchase a property, please use an agent. They have the expertise and the insurance to cover any issues that could come up with the purchase of a commercial property. In Colorado, being a real estate agent actually allows you to practice law without being a lawyer. After becoming an agent, you can specify a distinction in residential or commercial.

Here are a few things to consider before choosing a commercial agent:

- Make sure you hire a commercial agent for commercial properties, obviously.

- Ask what their experience is in off-market deals, also called pocket listings. (These are listings of properties, well, actually non-listings, and that's the difference. These properties aren't on the open market yet, so competition is often lower.)

- Ask them how long it takes them to return a phone call or e-mail, so you know if their timing works for you. (And pay attention to being responsive yourself; timing is critical.)

- Ask what market data they rely on to know if a property is a great deal. (You should hear things like demographics, sales comps, price per square foot, and rental comps.)

- Ask about their experience and how long they've been doing this.

- Ask if this is their full-time job.

- Ask if they have any experience in the marijuana industry.

- Ask for at least three referrals, and ask these questions when you reach out:

- Would you use this person again?

- What was the deal you did with them?

- Were you satisfied?

- What was the best part of working with this agent?

- What was the worst part of working with this agent?

- Would you work with this agent again?

- Anything else I should know?

- What are the terms of a contract to work with them?

- Have they won any awards or gotten any recognition for their work?

This can be a complex process, and you don't want to

get involved with a property, a lease, or a landlord that will cause you problems. Be thorough and get advice from people who know their stuff. Moving a location is a huge cost that you should try to avoid. Get it right the first time.

COMIN' HOME

LYNYRD SKYNYRD

Designing Your Space

WHAT IS (HOPEFULLY) GREAT ABOUT BEING AT HOME? You are in an environment that you created, with nice décor, pictures, and things you've collected throughout life that have great stories behind them. Most of all, you are calm, relaxed, and comfortable. When you are comfortable and relaxed, you are more open. When you are more open, you connect more easily. That is why we want to create an environment at your location that feels like "Comin' Home." We do that physically (the store) and emotionally (how people feel in the store).

I was in a store the other day, shopping and observing the environment. Everyone was thinking about breasts, G-strings, sex, and future engagements, and it wasn't an adult entertainment store. It was a place that had great lighting, upbeat music, darkly painted walls, clean floors, cool artwork, attractive and helpful staff, and lots of product. Any guess? It was Victoria's Secret. I thought, "Wow, they have taken something so personal and intimate, and made it rather comfortable." I had to know how this got started.

Roy Raymond and his wife Gaye founded the company in San Francisco on June 12, 1977. The idea started from a single uncomfortable experience Roy had while shopping at a department store. He was looking for lingerie for his wife and was faced with racks and racks of terry cloth robes and ugly floral print nylon nightgowns. He said he always had the feeling that the saleswoman thought of him as an unwelcome intruder, so he studied the lingerie business for eight years, borrowed $80,000 from his parents and $40,000 from a bank, and opened a single store where men would feel comfortable buying lingerie. The store grossed $500,000 the first year, and it now sells products in more than forty countries. The name "Victoria" came from Queen Victoria, and the "secret" was hidden underneath the clothes.

Creating a welcoming, safe, and comfortable environment in a retail space is essential, especially in the marijuana industry. Imagine a person you think might feel the *least* comfortable in a marijuana dispensary and consider how you could make that person feel at home. If you've done your market research, you might even have a good idea about who that type of person is in your area. Use the person as the bar for comfort when you plan your physical and emotional environment. You're going to be able to do something special after you read this book (and with my support): you'll have a consistently excellent product, authentic employees to assist customers, *and* a comfortable environment in which people can shop. When people feel good, they buy more and want to come back more often.

Here are a handful of elements you should consider, but above all, design with your customer in mind and in alignment with the values and image you want to project. Your space is a physical symbol of what you represent – don't underestimate its importance and impact.

OUTSIDE THE BUILDING

It's got to be clean. Basic. Pressure wash the building, the entry-way, the sidewalks, the parking lot, and everything you can to make it look better. It shows that you care. People notice details. If you bought the building, paint it if needed. Have the windows cleaned every two weeks. Have the trash picked up every day. If you have planters, or plants and trees, make sure they look good, trimmed up, and freshly mulched every year. If you have a handrail on the stairway, make sure it is painted and clean. Many medical and recreational stores are open as late as midnight. Make sure the lighting makes the area feel safe at night, and that the walk from the parking lot to the building (if there is one) is as smooth as possible to avoid tripping (if a customer is coming to you because of a medical need, you want to ease the person's physical experience in any way you can).

Lastly, it's important for people to feel safe. Do you think it would help someone feel more comfortable if there was a security guard there? You bet – just be sure the person you choose is trained to make people feel that he or she is there *for* your customers, not *because* of your customers. There is a difference between having an armed security guard who looks like he's trying to make the SWAT team and a security person who makes a customer feel comforted.

When a guard is all decked out in gear, it makes customers feel like there is something to be afraid of (more than they thought). Instead, a security guard could wear a clean uniform and a clearly marked security jacket or shirt. Think of the folks who guard the field at sporting events. They are just there to make sure you don't go past them. Also, lifeguards at pools are there if you need them and they're watching things, but you really only notice them when you need them.

ENTRANCE

Again, clean. You wouldn't go on a first date with stains on your clothes, and it's the same thing here. First impressions matter. It would be ideal, depending on your layout, to have space for people to "land," meaning you don't want the first five feet slammed with products and overwhelm customers. Customers tend to go to their right, so follow IKEA's example and have a path laid out that takes advantage of people's natural tendencies. What goes with marijuana? Vapes, pipes, and bongs. Have these items in glass display cases and beautifully lighted, if possible. The lighting will make the vibrant details in the products pop, and they will look like art.

As mentioned earlier, if you're planning to gather information from customers before they shop so that their salesperson can better assist them, it's important to have a space for this near your entrance – it immediately signals that you are interested in serving their specific needs. Additionally, if you are posting any friendly "ground rules" for your store, make sure they are visible at the entrance.

Finally, if you can afford it in your staffing model, it's a great practice to have someone (beyond security) at the entrance to greet people and give them a quick understanding of the store and how to get help with their purchase. One comfort issue in a dispensary is that many customers haven't gone to one before, or they are still nervous about going to one. A greeter helps put them at ease so they don't feel lost or uninformed.

LAYOUT

Ideally, you want people to move through the store to potentially pick out additional products and have more time to look around. Also, if you have items around the perimeter, it will help pull people in. There is a delicate balance with these extras. You don't want to make it difficult for people to get in and get what they want, but you want them to maximize their purchases. After you finish your initial setup, get a few friends or family members to come to the store and imagine they are there to shop. Get their feedback on the flow of the space and how it felt to move through it. Does it feel clear? Does it feel smooth? What catches their eye? Can they read any signage they need to see? Do any bottlenecks occur when there are a lot of people in there? Can employees and customers easily hear each other as they interact? If you're stuck on ideas for how to create your layout, go to stores where you feel comfortable and that you frequently visit. Think about what they've done and how you might model your store in a similar way.

SALES COUNTER

You may have heard about the psychological barrier of sitting across the desk from someone. If you are across the table (or desk or counter) from someone else, you are literally on opposite sides. The idea to remedy this situation (when it isn't desirable) is to take your chair and move it to the side of the desk or table to get closer together physically and remove any barriers. Now, you can't fully do that in a retail space, but you can have counters that are smaller in length with more openings for employees to come around and stand with the customer now and then. You can also make sure your counters are the right height to make interacting over them still feel personal. You don't want your furniture to create an "us vs. them" environment.

BATHROOMS

This should be the most obvious place to keep clean (think: the opposite of the bathroom at PopCopy from Chappelle's Show). I've never known anyone who has gone to a front counter to let the manager know the bathroom is not up to standards. It's not our customers' job to let us know this; we need to be on top of it. While it's not visible to every customer, a clean and comfortable bathroom lets people know you care about the details and makes your store feel even more trustworthy (we value what's on display and what's behind the curtain). Have a rotating schedule to check and clean the bathroom and make sure it is right. It has to smell clean, include a piece of art, display the right lighting, and offer a clean floor, sink, toilet, and mirror. Towels and toilet paper must always be stocked.

SIMPLICITY

You want to create an environment that makes it as easy as possible for people to do business with you. For example, you will likely have locked display cabinets with different keys. The last thing you want is to be fumbling around looking for keys to open a cabinet for someone to see something up close. A person asking to see something is obviously interested in buying. Don't ruin the momentum by not being ready. If everyone does not have a key to all display cases, have them numbered and place the keys in a designated space, close by.

DECOR

Think high-end and high quality. You don't have to reinvent the wheel here. Go to high-end hotels and restaurants in your area, and take notes. They have paid a lot of money to designers to figure this all out for them. You may not want to spend money on a professional designer, so find professional designs you like elsewhere and create the look and feel you want in your store. My dispensary featured dark hardwood floors (tile is a good, less expensive, more durable alternative); lighted artwork on the walls; rich, dark colors to create warmth; and two large leather couches if people wanted to get comfortable.

EMPLOYEES AND UNIFORMS

Being a former athlete, I like uniforms (or at least a clear dress code) for a few reasons. Remember that for many people, marijuana is a response to pain, and therefore the comfort of their store experience can come as a relief since they are already uncomfortable. (For example, at one dispensary, we had a separate area with a small table, a lamp, and three chairs for medical patient consultations. We took the time to fully understand people and their medical conditions and make recommendations). Also, as I have mentioned, this is a scary new world for some people. There is a lot of anxiety about entering a store like this. Some of the people covered on television related to this industry don't, frankly, look like serious business people (they look like potheads who are trying to be cool). Employee uniforms, or a dress code, put people at ease. You don't have to be "cool" to be a customer. Just be yourself so we can take care of you … that's the message you want to send.

I played college football for a strong team. In two years, we lost three games, and the head coach was crazy about the details of uniforms. If it were up to him, they wouldn't have even had different numbers because that separates players from one another. The point is this: studies have concluded that customers feel more comfortable and inclined to do more business with employees who wear uniforms because they stand out as professionals, and are seen as being more competent and knowledgeable. However, like a sports team, the aligned professional gear unites your staff and makes customers feel like they are getting taken care of by a team.

Can you imagine getting pulled over by a police officer wearing sweats? Or waiting at the gate for a flight, and the flight crew shows up with sloppy, mismatched clothes? Or going to court and the judge is wearing a tank top and a straw hat? Uniforms raise comfort levels and signal professionalism.

Here are the top seven reasons uniforms will benefit you and your employees:

- *Approachability*: You want your customers to feel comfortable knowing where to go for help, and you really don't want a customer asking a fellow customer for help.

- *Team Spirit*: Your team feels more together when they look similar. Uniforms connect them better to each other, which will allow them to support each other and provide a better overall experience for your customers.

- *Positive Image*: You know that people judge other people by how we look and what we wear. If you have a customer who is offended by something an employee is wearing, it will damage your customer's relationship with the business.

- *Easier*: Having a simple uniform program can take the pressure off of your employees. They know what is expected and it is easier to manage.

- *Promote and Advertise*: Having the name of your business on clothing will help promote the brand, and seeing it more will help people remember it. Additionally, when your employees are not at the store, they are walking billboards for your business, and could easily be approached with questions and conversations.

- *Pride*: When you join a team, it should feel significant. You're not just showing up to work; you're a part of something. The uniform cements the fact that your employees are part of something new and will be excited about it.

- *Ice Breakers*: Another detail about uniforms is the name tag. The name tag is the ice breaker. There's a guy named Scott Ginsberg who has worn a name tag 24/7 since the year 2001 and counting, and he's learned something amazing. Just by knowing someone's name, it opens a door. You can skip the part about, "What's your name?" but mainly, it takes a few bricks off of each person's wall. Someone feels like they know you better already. You can also add something to it that gives it more personality. For example, name tags of employees can include the person's favorite movie, favorite actor, hometown, dream vacation, favorite food ... anything to get employees and customers more quickly into an easy relationship.

Now, you might be thinking, maybe even sarcastically: "Team spirit? Pride? Fat chance. Haven't you seen all the articles about millennials and how they don't want to work hard and they want it all now?" Blah blah blah, if you don't believe me, do me a favor and go to a Chick-fil-A just twice, once in the drive-thru and once inside. There are plenty of young, bright-eyed people in uniforms who have pride and are also professional, efficient, and extremely friendly. I've been to a lot of great restaurants, and Chick-fil-A rivals many for consistent service. They greet you by name when you pull up to the window to get your order. Also, don't think for a minute it's lost on employees how much money the company loses by being closed on Sundays. People choose to work there, in part, because it's a company that's willing to make sacrifices to stay true to what it values.

If you are thinking, "Wow, this is a lot of work," you're right, it is. But we're not talking about being a half-ass operator making money in the short term. Look, if you have the only ice cream shop on the beach in the summer, do you think you are some great salesperson who's a genius for selling something cold to people who are hot? No. But if you have an ice cream shop on the beach, near four others, and you have the most revenue and the happiest customers, now you are doing something. You're succeeding by creating the environment that your customers want. And that is what we are going to do.

EYE IN THE SKY

THE ALAN PARSONS PROJECT

Commercial Security

COMMERCIAL SECURITY IS HIGHLY INVOLVED. There are many aspects, from managing customers and employees to managing your real estate, product, and transportation. I recommend that you contract this to a company that works with other businesses (or perhaps you see an opportunity to start a security business to serve the marijuana industry). Here are things to consider when looking at security companies:

- What data do they have on customer satisfaction with security?

GET EDUCATED — THE BUSINESS – THE BASICS

- Do they have data on their effectiveness (number of security breaches, issues with personnel, etc.)?

- What is their philosophy on their guards' customer service? How are they trained? Are you allowed to be a part of choosing/hiring people?

- What technologies do they use for real estate and product security?

- Do they offer any liability coverage for breaches in their system or with their guards?

Ultimately, make sure you call references and/or visit the locations they say that they secure and get a sense of how they operate.

GOING MOBILE

THE WHO

Safe Product and Cash Transportation

HAVE YOU EVER SEEN A PRESIDENTIAL MOTORCADE? Motorcade is absolutely the right word for it. The definition of motorcade is: a procession of motor vehicles. I've seen it a few times, but the last time was when President Obama was in Colorado for a debate, and I was trying to get on the freeway in the morning. The exits were blocked by motorcycles, and the freeway was shut down for at least ten minutes. Then, with no cars anywhere around, a blaze of lights and sirens comes barreling down the freeway. There were fifty motorcycles and twenty cars, then four Suburbans with all kinds of lights, and then the limo. It was incredible, but what was interesting is that I had the realization that all this protection seemed like it actually made the president less safe. They were advertising exactly where he was. If someone wanted to take a shot at the president from the freeway overpass, they would know right where he was.

What if, instead, they had him get in a random taxi? You'd never know where he was. And that got me thinking about transporting money and product in this industry. Trucks (armored cars and other tagged vehicles) identify where the money is for anyone who might want to try and steal it. Maybe it would be easier and more discreet to move it around if it was in a milk truck or some other misleading vehicle. Sometimes we can overwork something that would actually be better off being understated. For transporting money and product in this business, understated is safer.

Moving the product from the grow location to your store or multiple stores can be an opportunity for trouble. You can make it more difficult for opportunists. While someone has come up with a concept of using armored cars and other such vehicles, my solution is this, and it is a heavy solution. Buy a nondescript van with no lettering or fanciness, and then buy file cabinets (that are actually small safes) with individual combinations. Place the cabinets in the back of the van and weld a steel frame around the cabinets so they cannot be moved. Then give each store you deliver to a combination for the store's individual safe (if and when you have multiple stores). This way, the van can make deliveries from the grow location to the stores with very little risk from outside influences. Cash can obviously be transported from the stores to the main location safely in the same way.

INVISIBLE TOUCH

GENESIS

Packaging for Transportation and Sale

SHOULD YOU PACKAGE YOUR PRODUCTS AT THE GROW SITE or at your store? It's a tougher question than you might think, and here's why. It is easier and less expensive to prepackage at the grow location, but then the customer cannot smell the product. You might think that is not a big deal, but it's similar to buying fruit or fresh bread. Most customers want to experience that scent. And it's part of the culture, for sure. Stores have tried to overcome this by having a sample of what you are buying in a sample jar, but it is not what you are actually buying.

Some boutique stores have no prepackaging, and this provides a better, more organic experience. The trade-off is that it is more expensive to package product at the store, and it makes transportation riskier. Depending on the state you live in, you may not have to make this choice because some states are mandating prepackaging. In Nevada, for example, everything has to be prepackaged. Make sure you know the rules in your state before you settle on a transportation method and design for your store. This small element of your operational model impacts your business plan tremendously.

LEGAL TENDER

B-52S

Financial Forecasting

SIMPLE QUESTION:

What do you call someone who you love, but don't have sex with?

SIMPLE ANSWER:

Family or a very good friend.

SIMPLE QUESTION:

What do you call someone who you love, and have sex with?

SIMPLE ANSWER:

Your partner (husband, wife, girlfriend, boyfriend). Sex is really one of the main, if not *the* main, distinctions between your partner and other people you love. So think about this pairing ...

SIMPLE QUESTION:

What do you call something you spend a lot of time doing, but don't make money doing it?

SIMPLE ANSWER:

A hobby.

SIMPLE QUESTION:

What do you call something you spend a lot of time doing, and make money doing it?

SIMPLE ANSWER:

A business or profession.

Money, like sex, is a major differentiator in how you spend your time. So, just like sex in a relationship (at least good sex in a good relationship), you have to focus on it enough that you get the results you want, but you don't want to let it be at the center of everything. As I described in the pricing chapter, you need to plan thoughtfully around your revenue and expenses, as the balance will ultimately be what makes you money, but you can't do that at the cost of running a strong business focused on caring for your people. The way to achieve this is through thoughtful financial forecasting (and then financial upkeep) that will ensure you have a plan and have worked through contingencies so you can focus on the other elements of the business.

Carefully creating financial plans, when you are in a thoughtful and centered place, will help you make smart money decisions when you're more stressed and/or emotional as things get underway. Take a lesson from Mr. Ryder, and keep emotions and money as far apart as you can.

Financial statements are the guide that can make or break your business in the eyes of potential investors, and, most importantly, they will tell you what the real potential of your business really is.

When you sit down to think about it, consider how you approach your own home budget. If you need more money in your budget at home, there are only two prudent things you can do: cut expenses or make more money (or a combination of the two). Business is the same. Start with your anticipated expenses because you have the most control over those.

SAMPLE LIST OF EXPENSES

- Mortgage / Rent
- Utilities
- Property / Rental Insurance
- Telecommunications: Internet, Hosting, Cell Phones
- Salaries
- Employee Insurance
- Taxes
- Legal Fees
- CPA Fees
- Office Equipment / Supplies
- Marketing
- Advertising
- Training / Education
- Cost of Goods Sold

As you plan for how your revenue will offset these expenses, and of course, outpace them such that you have a profit, remember to estimate your best-case scenario, as well as a more conservative one. Additionally, you might want to create a forecast for several different stretches of time (one year out, five years out, etc.). Luckily, we live in an age where smart financial folks have created online businesses that provide tools for people like you and me to use in doing this kind of work. I like SCORE.org, as it offers several useful resources. As you get ready for this stage of your planning, check it out and use it to get you started.

TAXMAN

THE BEATLES

Managing Taxes and CPAs

TAXES ARE TRICKY IN THIS INDUSTRY FOR A FEW REASONS. This is still federally illegal, and there are only a handful of accountants/CPAs that will take on the business. However, I ONLY DO MY TAXES WITH A CPA for a couple of good reasons.

First, the relationship with your accountant is likely as important as the one with your spouse. Okay, maybe not your spouse, but for sure your lawyer. Why? Because accountants know all the rules about taxes and money, and money is the purpose of your business, right? (Money is the tool that gets you to your why). Second, your odds of getting audited are extremely low if you use a CPA (less than 1 percent). Now, if you make over $10 million a year, your odds will go up to about 16 percent, but good for you. I'd deal with that every year. Either way, you want to have someone in your corner who knows the rules and can ensure your finances hold up against scrutiny if you get audited. Common sense tells me that if I file as an individual (by myself), I'm the one who will gain if I make mistakes in my favor. So, if I were the IRS, I would look more closely at those returns. When a professional files your return, the CPA basically certifies with his or her experience and license that your return is correct. Do you think that a legitimate CPA would risk a license just so you can cheat a little? It's not worth it. I believe that the IRS knows this, and therefore spends less time auditing taxes submitted by licensed CPAs.

An accountant can help with many things in addition to taxes. Let's start with three terms to ensure you are clear on the different types of financial management you might need and use:

BOOKKEEPER

Bookkeepers work on the short-term finances of the business. They work with the day-to-day details by recording all the financial events. This will obviously make the accountant's job easier if it is done properly.

ACCOUNTANT

Accountants work with the long-term finances of the business. They analyze the recordings of the bookkeeper and report back to you.

CERTIFIED PUBLIC ACCOUNTANT

CPAs are more qualified, tested, and experienced versions of accountants. Licenses depend on individual states, but the base requirements usually include a bachelor's degree, two years of experience in accounting, passing a state exam, and periodic retesting. They can also perform more complex tasks like audits.

Software has replaced the essential duties of bookkeepers, but CPAs are still worth the investment. Let's take a quick run of the many types of finances you will encounter running a business:

- Financial forecasting for the business plan and any loans.
- Daily expenses to manage, track, and pay.
- Cyclical bills that need to be paid and accounted for.
- Bank statements to justify against your returns.
- Records for tax purposes.
- Records of accountability for anyone who has invested in you.
- Taxes.

Before you form the company, you'll want to sit down with a few CPAs and ask them questions about which way is the best way to set up your company's legal status (even though you know a lot about it now), based on your goals. Plus, it is a good way to get a feel for each CPA to see which one you want to do business with.

Conclusion: If you have the right software, you can replace the bookkeeper's job easily, and then make it easy for a CPA to handle the big stuff. If your budget is tight, find a way to make it work and hire a CPA anyway. Remember, the overall point here is to start right and run right, not start flawed and end broke. Okay? Also, you don't want to spend a lot of your time doing things that are not core to your skills (and most of us are not accountants). Do you think Elon Musk or Warren Buffett are doing their own taxes? No.

Here's the advantage of working with a CPA, and what they can do to help you:

TAXES

They prepare the returns. My guy calls me after we meet and tells me what I'm getting, and sends me the returns. I sign them and send them back in the postage-ready return envelope, and it's as easy as that. They can also help if you are doing business in multiple states and with internet sales. Interest from short-term debt needs to be written off correctly, or it will cost you more. Tax publications are available from irs.gov for free, but these people know what is best. For example, you might think having an office at home is great, which it is, but if you use that as a business write-off, then you cannot use the maximum of your home interest write-off. Either one may be right for you, but it is better to have someone explain the options and the advantages and disadvantages of each, instead of guessing.

BUSINESS SETUP

You know enough to be dangerous, but picking the legal structure is important. It is the basis of your foundation. Plus, as you make this decision, you must consider many things that will have critical implications. For example, how the business is set up could affect your health insurance policy for your employees.

ADVICE

Now, no one but a few saw the 2008 economic "depression" coming, when over $22 TRILLION was wiped out of the US economy, and the federal government had to rescue the big banks. Your CPA can provide a valuable set of eyes, not emotionally attached to your business, to see the big picture and look at financial trends. Do you think numbers people look at other numbers besides yours? Yes, they do. They can see things that you might not see while working in the day-to-day operations of your business.

CHECKUP

You go to the dentist and the doctor for checkups, you take your pets and children in for checkups, and you want to get a checkup on your business, too. CPAs have all the data. They can look at cash flow, payroll, inventory, sales, and profits, and share valuable advice on what you should do.

PREPARING FINANCIALS

Financial statements are the report cards of your business. Like I said, a corporation is considered a person, and this is his or her report card. Clear, clean, and certified financials are a game-changer for:

- Loans: CPAs will help you determine the advantages and disadvantages of getting a loan and what effect that would have on taxes.

- Unverified statements: They will put together statements based on your input.

- Semi-verified: They are familiar with your company and industry and can provide a formal report of the statements.

- Fully-verified: CPAs will verify the accuracy of your numbers, and examine bank accounts, assets, and inventory. This is helpful when you are considering selling or merging your business.

QUESTIONS YOU WANT TO ASK A CPA

- If I'm working with a firm, will I be working with the same person every time?

- If I'm working with an individual business, what is the availability of the CPA's time and what is the best way to communicate?

- How do you get paid (retainer, monthly, hourly)?

- What are your rates?

- Are you okay with me submitting information in a software program?

- How many clients do you have?

- Do you have references?

- Do you have any experience in the branch of the industry I am starting in?

- What is your favorite movie and why? (Just kidding, but you are starting a relationship here, and you want to make sure you like each other.)

The top eight mistakes new business owners make with taxes:

- *I have my own business, so I can pay myself whatever I want. It's all my money, right?* If you are incorporated, no you cannot. Let's say you pay yourself $60,000 to start, and then things are going so well you decide to pay yourself $120,000. The IRS could determine that because you doubled your salary from one year to the next, there has to be a substantial reason for that, and you could be responsible for paying corporate taxes on the increase.

- I *can do this all myself.* I've seen the commercials for the many tax services. I'm not saying that you can't go that route. I'm saying that with the consequences being so high, you might want to start off right. Also, have you heard the statement from Abraham Lincoln, who was a lawyer? He said, "He who represents himself, has a fool for a client." Don't skimp on this.

- *I have QuickBooks. Do I need a tax organizer?* A tax organizer is basically a place to store every number you need to file in your taxes. This is also a great place to hold all your documents. Even though we are getting more and more paperless, we still generate a lot of paper. It is way easier to have things in one place than to try and dig them up from all over. With QuickBooks and a paper copy, you'll always have everything you need and backed up in a rudimentary form, too.

- *You run tight on cash or want to borrow from employee withholding.* When I was in real estate, we had trust accounts, and they are called trust accounts for a reason.

The idea is that the money is trusted to be put aside and not to be touched. It is a mistake to think the money being set aside is really your money. It isn't. You don't want to be personally liable for getting into trouble with this. Just don't do it.

- *You get a huge refund.* You don't want to get in the habit of lending people money for free. If you get a huge refund, that is what you are doing – lending to the government. There are all kinds of sales in the marketplace, "Hey, come and spend your refund with us, for this!" If this is you, have your CPA look at the numbers and make the adjustment. You want to owe a little or get a small refund. That is the sweet spot you're after.

- *Why have employees?* You may have heard about the largest ride-share company where the execs thought, "Hey, let's make everyone a contractor!" because employees are expensive. True, but if people are not employees, they determine when they show up, what days, what time, where, when, and when any job will get completed. The government ruled against this company, and if they did that to them, they will do it to you, too. There are huge penalties for not collecting employee withdrawals, Social Security, and taxes.

- *You don't do the books, but it's alright.* It is easy to steal from businesses, and you should be watching your employees more than the strangers coming through the door. If you have someone doing the books for you, entering all the information in QuickBooks, let's say, ask the CPA how much it would cost them to randomly review the numbers for you. Another way is to switch people so there are a few sets of eyes on finances. There are countless stories about businesses being ruined by thieves, and it can happen quickly. It's your money. Don't let anyone take it from you.

- *I went to dinner with my buddy and we talked about business after we left. Deductible?* Technically, yes. But you don't want to take advantage of this and abuse it. Not because it's the government and they won't really know, but because you are a person of integrity. You are going to have all that you want. Think big, fulfilled. Keeping things tight in your life will pay off more than a $100 dinner. Oh, and you have twenty-four hours to discuss any business related to the dinner, so you should be able to legitimately pull it off.

You might be wondering why I'm pushing so hard on you having a CPA and getting started on the right foot. You got me: my brother is a CPA and I'm trying to push business to him. His number is (976) … just kidding, there are only two organizations that I don't mess with: the IRS and the FBI. Those folks play to win and have the power to crush you. So, I don't want to see you get in trouble.

Another major distinction between the marijuana business and other businesses is Section 280E of the IRS code. This article of the code forbids a business (dispensary) from deductions otherwise allowed as ordinary business expenses from gross income associated with the trafficking of Schedule I substances. Since this product is federally illegal, that is what you are technically doing – trafficking drugs. This started in 1970 and really was a weapon against people manufacturing unlawful drugs like opiates, meth, and heroin, but it still includes marijuana. Essentially, what it means is that you can only deduct Cost of Goods Sold (COGS) on the dispensary side, and other expenses through the grow facility (two separate companies). That is how most people set it up. However, there are a few other aspects to this that you and your accountant should be aware of, too.

A group called "CHAMP" (Californians Helping to Alleviate Medical Problems), which started in 1996 in Utah (just seeing if you are paying attention), obviously started in California. This is a long story about a court case, but the end result is that the CHAMP's guidelines can be used for medical dispensaries only. What this group did was charge a membership fee to members, and the fee covered things other than cannabis, such as caregiving and counseling. I said cannabis and not marijuana, because marijuana is technically the final product from the flowers, and cannabis includes anything that comes from the plant itself: CBD oil, shake, and hemp.

So COGS for a grow facility is easy. Everything you buy for that operation is deductible: clones, clone trays, lights, salaries, and mortgage or rent. When I was buying properties, I got a real estate license and started a real estate company to get money to buy the investment, then started a management company to manage the properties, and had each property in a separate LLC. I could then utilize all the available deductions and reduce my overall taxes as much as legally possible. Now, to be clear, you can't say, "Oh yes, IRS, my management company charges a million dollars a year to manage five properties." But you can find out the average cost of a management fee, and use that.

Here is how to apply it to this industry. The way a dispensary could reduce its 280E regulations is to split the dispensary into parts. In other words, you can separate 30 percent of the store for inventory, and you (the business owner) are the new inventory manager. Now 30 percent of those overall expenses are deductible. Also, you could start a management company that stores the product after it is dried in bulk, the dispensary pays the storage fee to the management company, and that is added to COGS. That means you will not have to apply the 280E to the whole operation, only 70 percent of it. Every state is different and you will have to research your state extensively, but this is a good start to get you thinking.

I don't want you to think I'm a jerk by saying this, but this is exactly why the rich get richer. In order to succeed in any game, you need to know the rules. Don't get mad at the players; learn the rules to win your game. Don't you also think there is a reason wealthy people make contributions to both candidates in a race? They want to be covered either way. The people who are elected can't win without campaign contributions, and when the candidates get elected, they feel at least some (or a lot of) obligation to repay the favor. If you are playing fair in an unfair game, you lose.

GET EDUCATED

THE BUSINESS — THE PEOPLE

LET YOUR LOVE FLOW

THE BELLAMY BROTHERS

Love People

THIS IS THE SHORTEST CHAPTER OF THE BOOK. Teddy Roosevelt once said, "Nobody cares how much you know until they know how much you care." When in doubt, don't sweat the technique, care for people in your sphere (customers, employees, and others) like they are your family. There *are* a lot of techniques to *enhance* your connection to people and your love of people. We'll talk about them in this section.

P.S. Loving and caring about people is the most authentic part of being human. This is what we are built for, so if you're having trouble doing it, address the block within yourself and move past it. If you don't, you won't succeed in all the ways you want, so let your love flow.

THE LEADER

THE CLASH

Strong Leadership

ALL THE CHAPTERS IN THIS SECTION WILL REQUIRE that you apply the personal reflections, vision, and planning from earlier in this book, and execute them with excellent leadership. Business is about taking care of and valuing people – so you better make sure you're being the leader people need. So what is most important in excellent leadership? Here is a list of qualities that are essential in a great leader:

- Strength
- Vision
- Integrity
- Unflappable

- Definitive
- Fair
- Inspiring
- Passionate
- Respectful
- Effective Communicator
- Leads by Example
- Curiosity
- **ACCEPTS FEEDBACK**

1. STRENGTH

You've got to be strong-willed to be a leader. There will be challenges and changes in this business, as in any business. You need thick skin. You will be there, working your ass off, and your teammates will criticize you, not show up for work, or quit when you need them. You have to be strong and keep your eyes on your WHY.

2. VISION

Vision can be described as being able to see a future that hasn't happened yet. You need a clear vision of what you want to accomplish with this endeavor. Get clear and concise so you can communicate that vision so your employees know it and so your customers will experience it. Visionary leaders inspire people, and meaningful vision makes people work harder toward an aspiration.

3. INTEGRITY

Integrity is often viewed from a judgmental lens. For example, "I'm on time, so I'm good. You're not on time, so you're bad."

This is how people weigh their actions against another's to prove their own worth. At its worst, integrity might show up as, "I'm late, but I have a good excuse, so it's like I'm really on time." That's someone who needs to believe they have integrity, so they use excuses to make it seem true.

Integrity is like a bicycle wheel. When a wheel has all its spokes and they are true, the wheel rotates straight. You get a nice, comfortable ride. The rim has integrity. It operates effectively. When a rim has missing spokes, or they are bent or out of true, the rim bends and will not rotate smoothly through the brake caliper. Its rotation is slowed and labored. You wouldn't go up to the rim in a judgmental way and say, "You're such a bad wheel." It's just not effective and it doesn't change the situation. As a leader, you must be a wheel with integrity and run a business that works like a wheel with integrity. Your job for yourself and the business is to focus on keeping the spokes in alignment by making the necessary adjustments – so things roll effectively and smoothly. Don't judge; it shuts people down. Just get things in alignment.

4. UNFLAPPABLE

Being unflappable is one of my favorite strengths. I don't care what is happening in the moment, what happened previously or how bad it is; I just keep on rolling. I see this strength play out as a parent, the most. If my son is having a tantrum, which happens, and I start freaking out in reaction to his tantrum, it adds fuel to his fire. So, I just act like it's no big deal and I totally mellow out. Eventually, he is able to use my calm to calm himself and comes out of the tantrum. If one of your employees comes back and says, "Hey, we lost five clients today," you should be authentic and say, "That's disappointing. Let's talk about what happened so we can keep the next five." But don't throw a tantrum. Staying unflappable not only helps your employees in the moment, but also sets an example that they will adopt when dealing with distressed customers: it's going to be okay, and there's always a way forward.

5. DEFINITIVE

When you make a policy change or a big decision in your business, it's likely that at least one person won't like it. You must be ready with how you are going to deal with that, and know when you will listen to dissenting opinions, and when you need to hold firm and lead with rationale. There's an old saying in sales: "Don't wait for a bomb to go off in or after a meeting. Defuse the bomb before anyone gets hurt." Meaning, if you hear something or especially feel something is a problem, don't ignore it. It's a bomb. Bring it up and defuse it. This is being definitive in facing issues, as well as showing your staff that you want definitive solutions to problems, not for problems to be swept under the rug. Again, the best leadership qualities impact your work and set an example of that quality for others.

6. FAIR

Being fair as a leader means making clear decisions about when things should be equal (the same for everyone), and when they should be equitable (tailored to what each person needs). Most organizations require both. When Phil Jackson coached the Bulls, he took a lot of heat for seeming to have slightly different rules for Dennis Rodman. For example, he was strict about being on time to practice with most players, but Rodman could show up late without much consequence. It was pretty clear to everyone that Rodman was a unique dude but he could seriously deliver at the most important times. If Jackson had pushed for Rodman to cross every "t" and dot every "i" in a traditional way, it might have stamped out the individual fire that made Rodman amazing in games. Now, I'm not recommending generally giving different rules to different employees, but I do recommend being aware of setting equal policies, while also refraining from letting those policies blind you when it comes to doing right by people to bring out their best.

7. INSPIRING

Inspiration is fleeting and can have a short shelf life. Great leaders can inspire, but they also know that their styles can get old, and they need to hold others up as inspiration to keep everyone engaged and feeling fresh. Good leaders inspire others, and great leaders inspire others to carry on that inspiration so it snowballs throughout an organization. Just as we talked about, this is a way to empower employees – not with trust and responsibility this time, but to execute on the critical soft skills it takes to run a business. You can do this in simple ways. Consider having each employee share a positive story every week about another team member who's doing a great job, perhaps describing how someone offered extraordinary customer service or how the warehouse crew supported the front-line people. Compliments made in front of others carry more weight than if delivered in private. Plus, this will help everyone see that your vision is working, and it will reinforce the positive. If you adopt this idea, it forces everyone to look for the good things happening all around the business, and communicate them to each other to feel the difference they are making collectively.

8. PASSIONATE

Being passionate is a little peculiar for me to talk about

because it's so ingrained in anything I'm doing. If you have a general excitement for what you are doing, and you should, you want to convey that to your team. And I'm not talking about being fake; I'm talking about being truly excited for where you are. Remember, it is possible for you to die in a car crash on the way home tonight (morbid, but important to remember). Do you want your last impression from a workday to be you half-assing it though a day or a meeting? No. Bring your passion every day, and apply it to the big things and the small things. It will make all the difference.

9. RESPECTFUL

Once, a guy walked into the car dealership where I was working, and he was wearing a T-shirt, flip-flops, and raggedy jean shorts. After two employees walked past him, a brave and respectful soul who was thinking about service, not just a shoo-in commission, finally asked him if he had been helped. He said he hadn't. "What can I do for you, sir?" asked the salesperson. The man replied, "I'm from Oakley, and I'm here to buy two Dodge Vipers for myself and Andre Agassi." They were $60,000 each. Being respectful of all people is one of the most basic values to have as a leader – whether those people are your customers or your employees. You are in the business of having your customers get what they want and pay you for it, as well as the business of empowering and supporting excellent employees. That's it. Be respectful to everyone you interact with, even if you don't think they will "qualify" as lucrative investments. Respect always pays off, and it's the reputation you want to have with customers and employees alike.

10. EFFECTIVE COMMUNICATOR

Being an effective communicator is key, obviously. If you have the vision but cannot explain it, you're sunk. Groups exist that can help you practice speaking in front of people so you get better at it, and more comfortable leading presentations and speeches. Here are a few keys to any speech or meeting: start on time, frame the message to your audience, keep it simple and to the point, practice before the meeting, maintain eye contact with your audience, and leave time for feedback and input. We'll talk in an upcoming chapter about getting feedback from your employees. Asking them about your communication methods is a great way to assess if you're building this leadership skill.

11. LEADS BY EXAMPLE

You'll want to be aware of leading by example at all times. In business, just like with children, everyone is watching you to see what you say, what you do, and how you react to things – and then copy you. The other day at a traffic light, my son was yelling from the back seat, unprompted, "Go, go, go dumb cars." Who knows where that came from? Whoops. But seriously, if you nurture customers to ensure they have a great experience at your store, and then when they leave, you say, "What a fucking pain in the ass that guy was," your employees will think a lot differently about you. They might agree with you about the customer, but you will seem fake. Even if you are just blowing off steam, don't do it. It's the same reason you wouldn't shit-talk your spouse in front of your children – it sets an example that it's okay. It's not. Things can get trying and stressful at times. Find a person, not one of your employees, that you can let loose with, like a coach, mentor, or good friend.

12. CURIOSITY

I'm going to get personal here, again, because it will resonate quickly. If you have been with more than one partner, sexually, you know that people are different. What one person likes, another person may not. And if you are committed to being a good partner, you will want to be curious about what your partner likes and then do that as often as possible. Right? Now, as we have discussed, you want to be curious about who your people are in your business, as well – both customers and employees. Figure out what makes them tick, and then deliver that. Being curious about people blends a lot of the other leadership traits we have named, including being adaptable and being respectful. People love it when you know them well enough to meet them where they are and respond to their needs. This is a great marketing strategy for your customers and an important management strategy for your employees. For example, you can yell at some people, and it will light a fire under them, but if you yell at other people, they will shut down. You need to know who your employees are to reach them with what they need and support them to perform well and be successful.

13. ACCEPTS FEEDBACK

Getting feedback from your employees, customers, and family is the most important of all the leadership traits, for this simple reason: what you think is right may not be right for them, and if you are serious about serving them, then you need to know what they want. Do you know the weirdest part of all?! They will gladly tell you if you only ask them. This is particularly important as you get to know your customers. For example, if I'm going into a liquor store, I usually know what I want and already have my mind made up about it. Any major distraction from that goal is wasting my time. I'm clearly not browsing, and I don't look like I'm there to learn about new things. If the owner wants to come talk to me and showcase his brilliance about wine by explaining all that he knows, then that is about him, not me. If you serve people what THEY want, they will do business with you and your relationships will be better, too. However, getting feedback from all these people also makes you a better business person because these folks have a perspective on your work that you do not have. Be humble enough to ask, be smart enough to listen, and act where it makes sense. We'll dive into this even more in the next chapter.

STOP ME IF YOU THINK YOU'VE HEARD THIS ONE BEFORE

THE SMITHS

Asking For and Applying Feedback

ONE OF THE MOST COURAGEOUS THINGS YOU CAN DO as a leader and as a human being is to interview people who really know you. Why? Because you need to know about yourself in order to be the best version of yourself, and most people don't have the opportunity to say those things to you in a safe way. Have you ever noticed the absolutely incredible, heartwarming, teary things people say at funerals and memorials? I'm always amazed, and I think right after they say it, "Did the deceased person ever know how much he or she meant to others in that level of detail?" I doubt it. Why? Most people need a structure or an "excuse" to actually say the most important things.

As a result, I got an idea when my brother turned forty. He knew a lot of people from around the world, and most adults aren't going to travel to America for a birthday party. So I thought about the next best thing: I reached out to these people and had them submit a story, note, photo, or anything that was positive and loving about my brother. I collected all these messages from about fifty people, copied them onto small slips of paper, and put them inside balloons. I put the balloons all around at his party, and he got to pop balloons throughout the night and read these special messages. Needless to say, he was blown away, and the most amazing part was that people at the party who didn't know any of these out-of-the-country friends were moved by the messages. It also caused them to reminisce about their own friends and family, and the effect was second to none. What allowed these folks to be so generous with their comments? There was a structure that made it "okay" to gush some honesty and generosity. (Many people have continued this idea, so please feel free to do the same with your loved ones. It is worth all the work.)

Now, if it requires a structure to share incredibly kind things, you can imagine that this is doubly true when you also want people to share tough things with you. You need to make it systematic, as well as safe, for people to give you feedback that can help you grow and lead at your best. Just like in sales, you need to create ground rules before you begin. This is not the time for you to get defensive or fail to reflect and act on what someone says after they are vulnerable with you and give you some gold-nugget feedback for your life. You need self-discipline and self-awareness to handle this, but if you do, it will blow you away.

Here is how you set the ground rules:

You: "I know we set aside half an hour for this conversation, and I want to tell you how much I appreciate your willingness to do this huge favor for me. What I want you to know is this: whatever you say here is between us. I will never use what you say to damage our relationship. Meaning, I will never throw this back at you in the future. The purpose of this is for me to be a better person and a better business leader. Since we work together (or since you know me so well), I'm excited to get your answers to these questions, and I want you to be as brutally honest as possible. Especially if you think what you want to tell me would normally be hard for you to say. Is there anything you are nervous about when it comes to giving me feedback?"

Them: "Not really, I hope what I say can be something that makes a difference for you and the business too." (Or if they are nervous about something, listen and try to offer ground rules that will ease those nerves.)

Here are twelve questions to get you started:

- Is there something I need to know about myself that you don't think I know?
  - If yes, how does this impact my work? Your work?

- Do you believe that I take responsibility for my actions at all times?
  - Do I make it possible for other people to own their actions?
  - Can you give me examples of when I did it well and when I did it poorly?

- Have you ever seen me adopt a victim mentality, or act like I can't impact an outcome?

- How do I (or how do I fail to) model our company values?
  - Can you give me some examples?

- Do you believe that I am humble and learn from my team and my mistakes?
  - If so/if not, can you give me an example I could learn from?

- Do I communicate clearly with employees? Customers? How could I improve?

- Do I motivate and inspire others? How could I improve?

- (Share the leadership traits in the previous chapter.) Which of these leadership traits are my strengths?
  - Where could I grow the most?

- Do I honor and listen to others' viewpoints, especially when they are contrary to mine?
  - Is there any way I could be better at this?
  - Have I ever failed to honor any of your viewpoints?

- Do I create an environment where people can have fun at work?

- Is there anything you want to contribute to the success of the business but haven't yet?

- Is there anything I have done to damage our relationship that I'm unaware of?

- Is there anything that I didn't ask that you believe I still need to know?

Add to or subtract from this list as you think it will help you understand your strengths and weaknesses. Not only does this help you get better, but you are also showing an interest in another person's thoughts and input. When that is sincere, it allows people to feel valued and appreciated, and it builds trust. This is the glue that can keep your employees engaged and working with you, not against you. The kind of conversation I just outlined is for a more formal time that you regularly set aside to connect with your people. Once you have set that tone and done a few rotations, start thinking about how you can build feedback into your daily work with employees, so they don't always have to wait for a sit-down conversation to give the feedback that's on their mind at any time. If your employees ultimately feel responsible for elements of your success, they will fully be bought-in to the future of their business.

SEPARATE / TOGETHER

A TRIBE CALLED QUEST

You Are a Person — Your Business Is Not

TO BE SUCCESSFUL, YOU HAVE TO BE ABLE to separate yourself from your business, even though you are completely intertwined with it on a daily basis. Remember that your business *is* something separate from you as a person, even though you are personally invested in it. The book *The E-Myth,* by Michael Gerber, does a great job of speaking to this idea, if you want to read about it in depth. Here is a short story that illustrates why it is so important to keep this in mind:

Here in Colorado, I once had a tenant who was from Louisiana. She made the best authentic, homemade gumbo from a recipe that had been passed down through the generations in her family.

I got to enjoy some, and it was great. She wanted to get started selling it right away because she had always dreamed about having a Louisiana-style food truck. She was so excited to get started that she didn't wait to take all of the steps we've talked about in this book. She just borrowed electrical cords, got a ton of Styrofoam bowls, a crockpot, and went out to a big park on one of the coldest days of the year and plugged it in to start living her dream. You can see it, can't you? It's a beautiful picture – someone living the American dream by scrapping every day, trying to get momentum for an idea and actually doing something about it. Many American dreams start like this. However, when your identity is too wrapped up in your business, it can be almost impossible to separate the business from you. Imagine if a customer said to my tenant, "Hey, this is okay gumbo, but it could use more salt." That might feel like an insult to her family and her heritage, and to her as a person who has put her heart into the start of her business.

Now, I'm not saying that if one person in one hundred gave her this feedback, that she should change the recipe, but she needs to be able to approach this business with enough separation from her personal life that she can hear and value feedback from her customers. Business owners need to see feedback as constructive and try it on. Remember, 94 percent of all small businesses have failed within ten years. Starting off without a proper system to succeed, and failing to listen to feedback and make adjustments, is often a miss for small-business owners who can't separate themselves from their business because they have poured so much into getting it off the ground. Part of valuing your people – customers and employees – is ensuring that you have positioned yourself to be able, ready, and eager to listen for ways you can get better faster.

Another way that you should separate yourself from your

business is to ensure your structure is not dependent on you. As you create your business plan and get up and running, ask yourself, "Could this business survive if I was out with the flu for two weeks?" This means creating a system that relies on your employees and empowers them to lead in your absence. "Can I take a week-long vacation?" Not only is this important to the health of your business, but it also signals to your employees that you trust them enough to position them in this way. If your team thinks that only you can get anything done, they'll also leave it to you to get everything done. Giving your people ownership and the support to execute that ownership will make them feel valuable.

COMMUNICATION BREAKDOWN

LED ZEPPELIN

Employee Empowerment and Customer Service

HAVE YOU EVER NOTICED WHAT IT COSTS FOR TWO PIECES of toast at a restaurant? Usually it's between $1.95 and $2.95. All you are getting is two toasted pieces of bread with butter and jelly. You can buy a loaf of bread for $1.95, and get an average of sixteen pieces. So why would anyone pay the same price for eight times fewer pieces of bread? The management and the service. As a customer, you go to a restaurant seeking a nice environment, someone to do the shopping and cooking work for you, someone friendly to bring you your order, and someone to clean up the mess. One of the things I hate to do when I'm a customer is manage the process when that is the only reason I was willing to pay someone instead of doing it myself. I believe that unmet expectations are the cause of all upsets, or as Shakespeare said, "Expectation is the root of all heartache."

Some customers will tell you when you haven't met their expectations, but a lot of them will just choose not to be a customer again – and maybe even tell other people not to (remember our chapter on social media?). The same holds true for your employees. When your employees have unmet expectations regarding their position or your leadership, they will leave as soon as they can. It's not the customers' job to manage their own service and pay for it too. Now, I'm not saying that mistakes and problems should never happen, but when they do, there should be a system in place to minimize them and resolve them quickly. One of the best ways to do this (similar to giving your employees ownership as described in the last chapter) is to give your employees the power to make changes and meet customer expectations as the need arises. This also makes them feel in control over their own experience and expectations in the role.

When I was in college, I worked as a service advisor for a car dealership. I had a forward-thinking manager who gave us control over how to manage customer relationships. We each had an account number to which we could charge anything in order to serve a customer. His thought was, "You manage the customer relationship – I trust you to take care of them and to do what is appropriate. If I have a problem with what you are doing, I'll manage you." In other words, don't come into my office and take my time and the customers' time to explain every situation when you already know the solution. One of the best things we could offer a customer who was upset was a complete detail of their car. It cost the dealership about $36, and we usually charged $129 retail, so it felt like a real value to the customers when their cars were washed, waxed, and spotless. They felt good when they left, and I felt empowered to manage my work and their experience.

Your employees will often know more than you about a lot of things because they hear and see a lot "in the field" and in the store. You need to teach them and develop them so they know their jobs, and then trust them to do their jobs. Make sure you think of your employees as assets in your business.

This process begins before you even hire anyone. You must understand what kind of leader you are and what approach you will take in working with your employees. Make sure you've thought through how you will communicate to potential employees about what it will be like to work for and with you. This has to be clear from the beginning before you even have employees because you are leading with a vision for the future. You don't want to be fumbling around when you interview potential employees, and the clearer you are about what it will be like to work in your business, the better people will self-select into work where they want responsibility and trust. The job market is competitive, so people have options, and you want them to choose you (and eventually, you want a reputation for being a great employer).

Note that employee theft is one of the biggest problems in business, and especially this one. It's worse from employees than outsiders, if you can believe that. This is especially true with a dispensary, where marijuana and cash are at the center of exchanges. You have to have an eye, and a number, on everything, and this should figure into your security plan. However, if you build a culture of trust and responsibility among your employees, they will be much less likely to be tempted to steal, since they will see the success of the business as their own success. When you take care of your people, they will take care of you.

NOT SATISFIED

ASWAD

The Real Customer Service

YOU KNOW THE OLD SAYING, "The customer is always right." Well, that was developed way back when large retail stores were just getting popular. Marshall Field, founder of the Marshall Field's department stores and others, developed this motto advocating that customer concerns and complaints should be treated seriously so that customers do not feel cheated or deceived. It is important to realize that this philosophy was a major advancement in thinking, since the position at the time was, "Let the buyer beware," and misrepresenting and lying to customers was common. In Germany, the modern saying about customer service is, "Der Kunde ist Konig," meaning "The customer is king." Believe it or not, in

Japan, the saying is similar: "Okyakusama wa kamisama desu," meaning, "The customer is god." I agree with all these sayings – not surprisingly, given that I'm advocating for you to always value people – but I also want to make sure you think about what these sayings really mean.

Being of service to people and taking care of them is the foundation of life. To do that well, you need to understand a fundamental truth about what happens when someone chooses to be a customer with you. A customer doing business with you, especially in the service industry, is all about that customer making an emotional connection to your business (your people and your product). This is the reason why customers who have a bad experience are likely to talk about it on social media – because in one way or another, they've been hurt. Therefore, the real key to customer service and loyalty is to take care of (and appeal to) your customers emotionally.

In the *Harvard Business Review* article, "An Emotional Connection Matters More Than Customer Service" by Alan Zorfas and Daniel Leemon, they share:

> *"Our research across hundreds of brands in dozens of categories shows that the most effective way to maximize customer value is to move beyond mere customer satisfaction and connect with customers at an emotional level – tapping into their fundamental motivations and fulfilling their deep, often unspoken emotional needs (for details, see our HBR article 'The New Science of Customer Emotions'). That means appealing to any of dozens of 'emotional motivators' such as a desire to feel a sense of belonging, to succeed in life, or to feel secure."*

They go on to talk about "high-impact motivators" that stand out among the hundreds of emotional motivators that drive consumer behavior. I listed ten of these high-impact motivators and named how you might make this emotional appeal in the marijuana industry.

- Stand out from the crowd: People want to project a unique social identity and be seen as special.
  - By participating in something that is federally illegal and on the fringe of public acceptance, customers can feel like they are doing something unique.
  - If you take the time to know each customer and cater to his or her specific marijuana needs, you will make them all feel special every time they arrive at your store.

- Have confidence in the future: People want to perceive the future as better than the past, and have a positive mental picture of what's to come.
  - Customers participating in the marijuana industry believe they are participating in something that is better for the world.
  - For medical marijuana consumers, your products may be their only salvation to a pain- or symptom-free future.

- Enjoy a sense of well-being: People want to feel that life measures up to expectations and that balance has been achieved, and they seek a stress-free state without conflicts or threats.
  - As you will read shortly, we compared it to alcohol and marijuana can give a "satisfied glow" and reduce stress.

- Many people will appreciate being able to solve problems through natural means that avoid pharmaceuticals.
- Marijuana is often aligned in people's minds with a "hippie era" that believed in peace and accepting others.

- Feel a sense of freedom: People want to act independently, without obligations or restrictions.
  - It will make many people feel free that they can state-legally purchase marijuana for both pleasure and as a solution to pain/symptoms.
  - If you've ever been in chronic pain, you know that the freedom any relief brings is immensely welcome.

- Feel a sense of thrill: People want to experience visceral, overwhelming pleasure and excitement, and participate in exciting, fun events.
  - As we have already named, participating as a customer in the marijuana world still feels fun and edgy for many people.
  - You can create an environment that makes customers feel like they are a part of a fun community. How do you make people look forward to spending time in your store?

- Feel a sense of belonging: People want to have an affiliation with people they relate to or aspire to be like, and feel part of a group.
  - Many customers will believe they are a part of a business that is doing good in the world – make sure you publicize and share stories about how your customer

community is thriving and living happier lives with your products.

- Protect the environment: Many people sustain the belief that the environment is sacred, and take actions to improve their surroundings.
  - Using natural products will make people feel this way. You can also use sustainable practices and share those with customers.
  - You can also help people see how they are protecting their body's environment by using your products.

- Be the person I want to be: People want to fulfill a desire for ongoing self-improvement, and live up to their ideal self-image.
  - Your products can help people get better results with physical problems in a healthier way.
  - Marijuana products can also provide a fun and relaxing way to calm down and be present in the moment.

- Feel secure: People want to believe that what they have today will be there tomorrow, and pursue goals and dreams without worry.
  - Let your customers know that you will be there for them and always have what they need. Coming to your store can be a source of calm for them.

- Succeed in life: People want to feel that they lead meaningful lives, and find worth that goes beyond financial or socioeconomic measures.

- Many people will feel that by supporting the marijuana industry, they are supporting a meaningful movement to help the world be better.
- If your products meet the physical needs of your customers, they will feel better able to live their lives fully.

Do any of these motivators have anything to do with features and benefits, styles, colors, sizes, and packaging? Fuck no. It's not the surface stuff that is driving our customers. So think about your customer service on an emotional level when you think about how to take care of them and keep them coming back. Not connecting with your customers is a monumental error.

Make sure any of your employees who work with customers understand this and are knowledgeable enough to support customers' needs so the motivators can come into play. A customer doesn't "feel secure," for example, if the person helping them can't accurately speak to the products.

Here are a few questions you and your employees should be ready to answer for your customers:

WHAT STRAIN SHOULD I GET?

There's a lot of confusion about what strain is best for someone. The names do not mean anything and people mix them up anyway. What is important about what someone chooses is the THC content, as that will greatly determine the effects on a person. Remember that THC is the component that makes people high. CBD content is the other important thing to know, as that is a part of the marijuana plant that has incredible medicinal power, and does not create a high. You can get people interested in the tastes or strengths of different strains you grow, but be sure they understand those two fundamental elements of what they are buying so that they experience the product as they want to.

WHAT IS THE BEST WAY TO USE MARIJUANA?

Three are three ways: inhale, apply, and consume:

Inhale
Advantages: This is the quickest way to get the effects into your system, either through lighting and smoking (pipe, bong, joint) or with an electric vape that has an electric lighter and oil.

Disadvantages: Smoking has health risks and can damage your lungs, and it is a more intrusive method for your surrounding neighbors. Even vapes, which seem like the best of both worlds for people who like to smoke, still have chemicals that are usually toxic. Smoking marijuana is not as dangerous as smoking cigars or cigarettes, but it is not without effect.

Apply
Advantages: Topical applications are great because they can be applied directly to an affected area (knee pain, back pain) without getting high.

Disadvantages: There is evidence that topical applications work, but not as well as the other two methods.

Consume
Advantages: This is a great method for people who don't want

to smoke or for people who have health issues. (If you have cancer, the last thing you want to do is smoke.) Plus, this product can be put into almost everything edible: brownies, drinks, cookies, cakes, and ice cream.

Disadvantages: You can consume too much. It takes the body up to forty-five minutes to feel the effects of edible marijuana. If you're impatient, you might eat two or three in that time, and then you are going to feel really sick. Edibles may be the best option, but you have to advise people to eat them as recommended.

More questions about the products that you should be ready to answer:

- Is this a sedative?
- Does it relieve anxiety?
- Is this an anti-inflammatory?
- Is this an antispasmodic (relieves spasms)?
- How does this affect mood?

As you invest in your grow, you need to learn these things about the plant types you choose and the products you will make from them. Here is very basic info:

THC AND CBD

THC and CBD levels are not necessarily related. The THC level could be as high as 20+ percent, while the CBD level of the same product is less than 0.1. This means the "getting high" component is really high and the medical CBD amount is very low, so it's obviously not a medical-based product.

Consider what system you can use to keep yourself and your

employees totally up to date on products and the leisure and medical purposes they serve. The emotional connection your customers make to your business will be based on your team's readiness to serve them.

FLY LIKE AN EAGLE

STEVE MILLER BAND

Organizational Culture

PART OF VALUING YOUR PEOPLE – employees and customers alike – is creating a successful and healthy culture for your business. An incredible example of an organization that did this impact-fully was the Philadelphia Eagles in their 2018 Super Bowl year. I'm going to admit right up front that I'm biased here. I've been a Philadelphia Eagles fan since I was seven years old (yeah, that's a long time ago). Why? Because I loved the Kelly-green color with the clean silver wings. I wish they'd go back to that uniform someday, but either way, they could finally say they are Super Bowl champions after the 2018 season. Technically, they won the NFL Championships before the first Super Bowl was played, but it seems like no one counts those. Anyway, you may be asking, "What does this have to do with business culture?" Well, one of the biggest reasons they won in 2018 is this: their culture.

I won't go on and on here, but this team faced a ton of adversity. Quarterback Carson Wentz, the league's leading MVP candidate, was injured for the year in Week Eleven. Darren Sproles, leading punt returner and running back, was out for the year in Week Six. In addition to that, they lost Jason Peters and Jordan Hicks to season-ending injuries as well. Their coach was only in his second year, and the replacement quarterback, Nick Foles, was an improbable replacement for Wentz. Given all of these setbacks, on paper, this team shouldn't have even made it to the Super Bowl, let alone win it. A strong culture can pull an organization through all types of adversity because a strong culture orients its people to respond to obstacles in an aligned and solutions-oriented way.

Here are my six rules for creating a great culture that I saw played out in the Eagles organization:

- Set a clear goal.
- Engage staff in living your values.
- Make acknowledgment the norm.
- Play to your team's strengths.
- Set the example.
- Be accessible.

1) SET A CLEAR GOAL

Setting a clear goal in football is easier than in many organizations: win the game, win the next game, win the playoff games, and then win the championship. But it's your job to have just as clear a goal and path laid out for your business, and ensure that all your people are aware of it and have bought-in to it. It doesn't work if it's not done as a team.

Doug Pederson was smart enough to set clear goals for the Eagles, beyond the obvious, and to go about the season in a specific way: be aggressive with play-calling, and playing to win. It seems simple that professionals would play to win, but most NFL teams honestly do not. That season, the Eagles went on fourth down twenty-six times and made the first down eighteen times. That's the highest in the league. Ask yourself, "If the leader is confident in his team and shows that confidence openly through his decision-making, do you think it gives the players a little 'umph' in their steps?" You're fuckin' right it does. This is one of the main ingredients to building the self-esteem of both children and adults. When you believe in people, have a good game plan, and put your ego aside to win the end game as a team, people will go with you to that end with all they've got. In the Eagles culture, the clarity was around the goal and how they would achieve the goal. Everyone was on board.

2) ENGAGE STAFF IN LIVING YOUR VALUES

You probably remember the national anthem protests. Malcolm Jenkins, the safety for the Eagles, first raised his fist to "draw awareness to disenfranchised people, communities of color, injustices around the country, and our criminal justice system." Chris Long, a defensive end for the Eagles from Charlottesville, Virginia, donated his entire 2017 base salary, worth a million dollars, to charity. He donated his first six game checks to fund scholarships in Charlottesville, and the remaining ten to cities in which he has played during his professional career. This could have been a major distraction for the team, but these players on the same team, who took different approaches, were able to support something bigger than themselves at a cost to themselves. The Eagles determined that their values as an organization revolved around standing up for something and going after what they believed in. That applied to their lives, as well as their professional commitments. If they had not been built-up to share that value, they might have ended up at odds since their passions for social change took them in different directions. Instead, they shared the values as a foundation for their connection, as opposed to the actions themselves.

3) MAKE ACKNOWLEDGMENT THE NORM

Acknowledgment is one of the most powerful tools we can use to build culture and tighten relationships. One reason is that it is used so little, and it is often not authentic. Newsflash: people want to be around people who make them feel better about themselves. Period. Most people aren't used to this type of culture, so they really value it when they find it, and it makes them more loyal and feel more aligned to the purpose of the business. Here is the farewell post from wide receiver Torrey Smith, who was only with the Eagles for a year:

"I would like to thank the entire Philadelphia Eagles organization for the opportunity to represent this city. Mr. Lurie thank you for being the man that you are and genuinely caring about your players and the people of the city. To all of the coaching staff, Thank you! Coach Groh thank you for your leadership and energy this season. I would like to personally thank Joe Douglas and Andy Weidl for believing in me since day one and treating me like family. We are family forever. I would like to thank my teammates, the men I will miss the most. I have never had this much fun playing this game that we all love and it was all because of y'all. We had a great time, worked our tails off, and made each other better. To my brothers in the wide receiver room I thank you! Groh and Press challenged us and we did it. WHAT A YEAR! We played for each other and because of that we will fly high together forever! I will miss G and the equipment staff, Pat and the video crew, strength coaches, trainers, pr team, SOME media folks (Someone tell Howard that Lebron is the GOAT), community relations staff, chefs, and janitors. I appreciate your friendship. I would also like to thank Duce Staley and Dom. Y'all are two of the realist dudes alive! Lastly to Philadelphia. Thank you for embracing my family and me. I look forward to visiting my family in PA for the rest of my life knowing that WE did it! They can't take that away from us! I have grown so much in my faith over the last year because of the men in that locker room. I will miss our Saturday night meetings and will always be grateful for that. Business is business and my time is up. I'm excited for another fresh start. Can't wait to see what God has next for me! One last time #FlyEaglesFly"

The Eagles organization valued its people, even when they were on their way out, and you can hear that throughout this excerpt from Smith.

After every game, Pederson would literally say, "You guys earned this. You guys did this. This is about you." His words were always to acknowledge the group as a team, and help them value their effort in each game. After the Super Bowl game, Pederson was asked about the quarterbacks, and he said, "You know, I think we could have won it with Carson if he was healthy, and Sudfeld (third-string QB) too." Although they hadn't played, Pederson never downgraded one player in order to glorify another.

Remember that payment is another form of acknowledgment, and you should think about how you plan to pay people, and if you want to ground some of that pay in performance (team or individual performance).

4) PLAY TO YOUR TEAM'S STRENGTHS

Another thing Pederson did extremely well, which was rather simple, was to have a coaching plan and plays specifically for each quarterback's strengths. When Carson was injured, the coach could have taken the easy way out and said, "Here is the plan. Go do it, Nick." Instead, he went back to the years when Foles had the most success in football and adjusted the game plan to make it easier for Foles to play well. It obviously worked. Nick Foles, who had been contemplating retirement only two years prior, ended up with pass completion numbers, a touchdown-to-interception ratio, and a win-loss ratio among the best ever. He also had the highest post-season passer rating in NFL history (with a minimum of seventy-six passes).

As we talked about in our leadership chapter, you cannot approach every employee the same way. Knowing your team members' strengths, and designing their work to maximize those strengths, will not only make you more successful, but it will make the team culture one where people feel seen and valued for their best selves.

5) SET THE EXAMPLE

Your behaviors will determine how people act and interact in your business – and this determines the culture. If you show your people (employees, customers, vendors) that you believe in them and care about them, they will generally rise to the level of expectations that you set by your example. People are longing to live a better version of themselves, and if you show someone you trust them, they will want to be trustworthy. Consider the many examples of great businesses that take former convicted felons and give them a chance to be the people they always could have been. Remember, everyone is watching you to see what you say, what you do, and how you react to things.

6) BE ACCESSIBLE

Recall from our leadership and feedback chapters that you need a structure to ensure you hear what you need to hear as a leader, and to help people feel that their voices matter in the outcome of the business. To stick with the Eagles examples, the best one I've seen was the Philly Philly, or Philly Special, a trick play called during the Super Bowl. At the goal line on fourth and one, Pederson called this play. My favorite part of the play is not just that it was successful, because things can go wrong and if you knew in advance which things would go wrong, you'd never make a mistake. The thing I love about this play comes out of the audio recording from the game. Pederson says, "We're going to go for it here." Foles comes over on the timeout and says, "Philly Philly?" Pederson hesitates for a moment and then responds like someone asked him to grab a burger after the game. He says, "Okay, yeah. Let's do it." Incredible. His ego could have easily taken over and insisted that he called the play so he could get the credit. Or he could have thought about the fact that it would be his ass on the line if they didn't make it, and choose not to take a risk. But he clearly built an organizational culture where people's input matters, and he had confidence in them. Foles was comfortable enough to suggest something risky, and Pederson responded in a way that made Foles confident it could work. That is the type of leadership that people want to work with.

Ultimately, the culture of your business is the atmosphere, the air, that everyone breathes. Its purity and health lead to the health of the team, and that allows the best environment for success, regardless of obstacles.

I'VE SEEN ALL GOOD PEOPLE

YES

Build Your Network

AN ADDITIONAL PEOPLE-ASSET THAT YOU HAVE, beyond your employees and customers, is your network. As you start your business, it is critical that you seek and sustain an active network that can support you, drive customers your way, and provide reliable advice and service. You would not believe the people you know, and who they know, if you push your thinking about who might be included in your network for this new industry. Many people are afraid to ask for help from their network, don't feel comfortable doing it, or don't want to damage a relationship by putting pressure on it. I have ideas for that.

First of all, most people like to help other people, especially if they believe you are sincerely interested in helping them, too. Have you ever thought about putting on a networking event? Imagine if someone you know called you and said, "Hey, I'm putting together a networking event for people who I trust and who have skills in their fields. Is that something you would be interested in?" I'm guessing your answer would be yes – it's flattering to be trusted and considered skilled in your work, and it's a good feeling to think you might be helping someone out. When I worked in real estate, I pulled in people who were related to the real estate industry who could help me, as well as each other, with all types of referrals. This network provided customer referrals, as well as referrals for other businesspeople with whom I could connect customers and trust that my customers would have good experiences.

Here is an example of a group I might have had at one of these events:

- Commercial agent
- Mortgage broker
- Home inspector
- Contractor
- Appraiser
- Property manager
- Moving company owner/manager

In the marijuana industry, you might seek a guest list like this:

- Real estate agent
- Lawyer
- CPA
- HVAC expert
- Electrician
- Plumber

- Construction industry contacts
- Web developer
- Public relations expert
- Marketing expert

Imagine how powerful it would be to have a group like this working together to support customers in this industry, as well as each other's businesses? If you're currently thinking, "I only know someone from one of these categories," then push yourself to reach out to family and friends to find out if they know and trust anyone they might connect you to. I bet you could start to generate a network if you dig deeply enough into your contacts.

Once you have a group assembled, it's important to get everyone on the same page. Share your vision, your idea about how you want to do business, your goals, and values – get them engaged about the direction you're heading so they can start to imagine how they might play a role in it. When you get into the tactical work of sourcing customers, make sure everyone understands the difference between a lead (bullshit) and a referral (real), because you don't want anyone to be spending time chasing down something that won't be fruitful.

Lead: Someone that the person loosely knows and thinks might be interested ...

- There is no foundation built to make this a warm handoff (where the customer is expecting the connection and knows a bit about you).

- There was no investigation from the referring person to see if the other person has any actual need in this area.

The person being called has no idea they were referred, or why.

Referral: Someone known by the person referring who has been prepared to expect you and needs your service/product.

- The referring person laid the foundation to make this a friendly, warm handoff.

- The referring person made an inquiry to see if there was even a need for the services.

- The person is waiting for the call from you.

If you are super short on customers and don't have any referrals, it doesn't hurt to explore leads, but actual referrals are WAY better. You may be asking yourself, "Why would someone go through all this work to give me a referral?" One reason is that if you make them feel like they are a part of a network where they can expect the same level of care in referrals, they will be eager to invest their time in providing referrals that meet this standard. Additionally, it isn't that much work, really. It's just having a few conversations with people you know who may be interested. Finally, meeting someone's need by referring them to you also builds goodwill between the referrer and the person being referred. Everyone wins.

I like to compare things to personal relationships because it clarifies things quickly, and nearly everyone can relate to it. For example, you would never recommend (refer) a potential date to a friend without letting both people know some background about each other. You wouldn't recommend (refer) a person for a date who was already dating someone or who was already married. And you definitely wouldn't recommend that someone call a friend to ask them out on a blind date without giving the other person a heads up that someone was calling. All of these situations would be awkward (for everyone involved). However, it doesn't take that much time or effort to provide an informed and warm introduction between two people that you think will have a mutual interest in each other.

Set an example for the network you are building around how to clearly ask for a referral so the person they are talking to knows how to recommend the right people. Instead of saying, "Hey, who do you know that could use my services?" (too generic and not well-thought-out), be as specific as possible. "James (a real estate agent), do you know anyone, or have any clients who could use some help *solving this problem* (name a specific problem your service/product provides)?" Lacking specificity puts the pressure on the person giving the favor, the referral, to do most of the work in thinking about who to connect you with. Bottom line: everyone in your network needs to make it as easy as possible to identify customers for each other. The same is true if you're generating referrals from personal contacts. For example, you might say to someone, "I know you golf at the club; do you think anyone in your usual foursome would need help with *this* (name specific problem)?" Bottom line: make it as easy as possible for someone to do you a favor.

Eventually, if you have built up a trusting network, you can also use each other to get help overcoming obstacles or needs that you have beyond generating customers. Networks are rich in expertise, or in connections to people who are rich in expertise. As an entrepreneur, building and valuing your network are essential to your success.

If you truly believe you don't have connections within your

current network of people, then you need to start attending networking events for business professionals in your area. These can be awkward and tough, but you have to get out there and build a network for yourself. Sometimes people will have a negative viewpoint about the marijuana industry, and there is a fun way to introduce yourself when networking. Here's what you do:

Them: "So, what do you do?"

You: (sheepishly) "You know I was afraid you were going to ask that."

Them: (shocked) "Really? You're at a networking event."

You: "I know, it's just that whenever I tell people what I do, they either want to find a polite way to walk away as quickly as possible, or they want some free samples."

(Now they are thinking, "What the fuck can this be?" The key here is they are likely thinking something worse than what you actually do, so when you tell them, it doesn't seem like a big deal. Additionally, you've captured their curiosity.)

Them: "Well, what the heck is it?"

You: "I own a marijuana dispensary." (Or "I'm an electrician who specializes in the marijuana industry," or "I'm a commercial grower in the marijuana industry.")

Them: (likely very curious) "I've always wanted to talk with someone in that industry. How did you get started?"

You: "I'm sure you've heard of the book *Weedonomics*. It's the greatest!" (Just kidding)

After talking with them for a while, you then get interested in what they do and see if you can make a connection that might be mutually beneficial in the future. Here are a few questions that can help you learn more about them:

- What attracted you to (their business)?

- What are you most proud of in your profession? (What someone is proud of reveals their core values.)

- What makes your company great? (Feel-good answer.)

- What is the craziest thing that has happened in your business? (A chance to tell a great story, which also reveals something about what/how they think.)

- Where do you see your industry going in five years? (They are a visionary.)

- What is a dream you've had related to your business that has already been realized? (They have accomplished great things and might have advice for you.)

- What is a dream for your business that is still in the works? (They have done so much and still want more; this might be an "in" for you.)

If you're a businessperson, then in some way, shape, or form, you are in the people business. Building a network is a part of that work as a source of referrals, business support, and mutual advantage.

WITH A LITTLE HELP FROM MY FRIENDS

THE BEATLES

Customer Referrals

ONE OF THE BIGGEST BLIND SPOTS FOR BUSINESS PEOPLE is often the opportunity for customer referrals, and I'm not talking about impersonal programs where people get a discount if they refer someone else. I know there are loyalty programs and cards and all that, but I'm not talking about a gimmicky bullshit program that is difficult to understand or see value from. You can use those techniques, but often owners concentrate on new business and growing the business, and don't spend enough time cultivating the people who are already customers. For example, I have one such card from an office supply company. I swear I have zero idea what the benefit is. Every time I purchase something, I can't tell any real difference. It seems and feels invisible. And if you are saying right now, "You should know; pay better attention to what it offers," my answer is: I shouldn't have to. That is my point. There should be an obvious connection to me, and what the benefit is to me, when I fill out some card with my information. Don't create a scheme that doesn't make an emotional connection to your customers or help them see exactly how the program values their loyalty.

Bottom line: you want it to be as easy as possible for your customers to do business with you.

Benefits and rewards should be obvious to THEM. If not, it's on you.

Keep in mind that people will gladly refer you to their contacts if you have helped them. They trust you and they like you (if you're doing the job we've just talked about). They are taking a huge risk if they refer a friend because if you don't take care of that friend, it will come back on them (the last thing you ever want to have happen). If you've done all that we have talked about in this book, you don't have to worry about that. You know customers will be satisfied, and their experience will greatly diminish the risk of referring someone else.

Here's how I address their potential concerns right up front (to blow up the bomb before it goes off):

You: "Jim, I appreciate you considering referring your people to me. I want you to know right upfront that I will treat them way better than we treated you (laugh out loud to lighten it up for him). No, seriously, you know I will take care of them. But I also want you to know I won't pester them. I just want to see if they are a fit for us. If they are, we'll move forward, and if not, we'll part as friends. Okay?"

Jim: "Sure, I trust you."

Do you know any good jokes? If you were in a casual conversation with others and someone randomly asked you to tell a clean joke, could you do it? It might feel like you were on the spot, and you'd have trouble with it. What would really be happening is that you would feel thrown off, maybe a little embarrassed (as if all you know are dirty jokes) and possibly not okay. The point is, it might be difficult in the moment. If you ask someone for a referral out of the blue, it's the same thing. They are on the spot, and if they can come up with a name, it won't necessarily be a good one. So don't put people in that position when you are asking for a favor.

Here is what I recommend:

If this is a customer who has a medical need, it is easy to dig deep for information and convert that into conversation points (example: they may be getting care somewhere, and you can ask if they know any other patients who might need your services). It may be a little more difficult with recreational customers, but if you spend the time getting to know them, you can find your "in." Let's imagine how you got Jim (from the previous example) to the place where you are assuring him that you'll take care of someone he has referred:

You: "Jim, I know you really like mountain biking."

Jim: "Yes, I've been riding for like ten years now. During the spring and summer, I try to get up there twice a month."

You: "That is great. Good for you. Do you have a group of people who you usually ride with?"

Jim: "Well, I ride by myself a lot, but there are a few guys who I go with occasionally."

You: "Do you think they would have any interest in what we have done for you?"

How would you know your customer likes mountain biking? You ask them what they are interested in during your interactions. Simple.

If you have the courage to dig deep within yourself and systematically dig deep with others (for them to get the most out of their lives), no one can touch you in life or business.

GET EDUCATED

CANNABIS – THE OPPORTUNITY

THIS IS IT

KENNY LOGGINS

The Opportunity in the Marijuana Industry

LET'S GET DOWN TO THE GREATEST OPPORTUNITY of our lifetime: the cannabis industry. The opportunity in marijuana is one of the most unique in American business and culture, and – if you're reading this – you're in the perfect spot to take advantage of it.

I'm telling you right now: there is a gold mine to be found in all aspects of this industry, and it can be a gold mine that you own, that you control, and – if you're growing marijuana – that you can replenish all the time. How long will this unique opportunity last? No one can say for sure, but I think within five years or less, marijuana will be federally legal and open to everyone. This is why you need to act today. For example, the state of Colorado has had state-legal marijuana since 2003, but it didn't really get rolling until 2006. Now it's off the charts with revenue, opportunity, and possibility. Those of us working in this industry in Colorado have already seen the flood of new participants, and while there is still room for plenty more in our state, you can see that the competition is heating up fast. One of the first states to legalize recreational marijuana, Colorado has had tremendous success with the program, and many states are following our example.

Interestingly, the last time in American history we had such a unique opportunity in a specialized market was during Prohibition. I believe there are important lessons to learn from how people capitalized on that situation at the time in order to generate opportunity and wealth. Prohibition, for those less familiar with it, lasted from 1920 to 1933, during which there was a constitutional ban on the production, importation, transportation, and sale of all alcoholic beverages in response to growing concerns about alcoholism and alcohol-related violence. In effect, the ban removed the regulation of the alcohol industry, making room for a huge "underground" industry to develop so that people who wanted to could still drink. Obviously, not everyone agreed that alcohol was dangerous.

So what is possible when you have a populace in disagreement with the federal laws and a business industry aching to thrive? Well, I give you one of America's most famous, wealthy, and powerful families: the Kennedys. The first son in the Kennedy family, Joe, died in WWII; the next son, John, was a President; the third son, Robert, was the Attorney General; and the last son, Edward, was a Senator. Their family is worth millions and millions of dollars. The alleged story behind that wealth is that the father of these men got started and made his real money during Prohibition as a "bootlegger." What we know speaks of a man who lived at the right time, saw an opportunity, took action, and made a fortune.

Noah Rothbaum wrote an article for *The Daily Beast* called "The Myth of Joe Kennedy's Bootlegging." He states, "What is true is that during the waning days of Prohibition, Kennedy traveled to Europe with Franklin Delano Roosevelt's son James, who helped him obtain importing contracts for Dewars, Gordons Gin, and Haig & Haig. James's presence next to Joe at business meetings signaled to the British business leaders that if they wanted to please the new administration, here was a good way to do it. Somerset Importers, Kennedy's company, got permits to sell medicinal whiskey in America, too, which allowed Kennedy to sign the importation agreements legally. Prohibition was repealed soon after his trip, leaving him in the perfect position to supply a thirsty America with high quality booze from the UK."

Sound familiar?

Kennedy wasn't a "bootlegger," he was smart and made the right moves at the right time. Was he obviously well connected? Yes, but now you are too.

When *Fortune Magazine* published its first list of the richest people in the United States in 1957, it placed the elder Kennedy in the $200–$400 million group ($1.7–$3.41 billion in today's money), meaning it estimated him to be between the ninth and sixteenth richest person in the United States. If you position yourself right in the marijuana industry, you can be in the perfect place to reap the rewards when it eventually becomes federally legal (which it will).

You might wonder why I'd hope for marijuana to become federally legal, given the advantages that can be had currently from the gap between state and federal laws. To illustrate why I want this, imagine if the NFL, NBA, MLB, and MLS all announced that they weren't going to officiate the games anymore. If the NFL said, "We're just going to let the players call the penalty on themselves. We trust that this will lead to a fair outcome for all involved." You'd immediately know that it was bullshit. If you follow the NFL, you'll remember well when the officials went on strike and the "scrubs" were brought in. After much criticism, nothing was done to fix the situation until the end of that Green Bay vs. Seattle game where the last call was so bad that it wrongly won the game for Seattle (dubbed the Fail Mary because it was so egregious). The NFL knew it had to do something. THE next day, the NFL and the "real" officials hammered out an agreement, and that was that.

The government is the marijuana industry's version of an NFL referee. We need the government as a referee because they are the only ones who can put people in prison, and that means they have people's attention. Ask yourself:

- When was the last time you bought food at the store and wondered if the label was correct? Thank you, FDA.

- When was the last time you got on an airplane and wondered if it was safe? Thank you, FAA.

- When was the last time you called 911 and no one answered? Thank you, FCC.

Almost never. These are the benefits of government. I'm not saying our government is perfect by any means, but there are useful elements of it that we all enjoy every day. Federal legality will make products safer for users, allow business owners to use banks and financing more easily, and offer protection from future monopolies coming into the business and edging everyone out. Keep in mind, part of the opportunity you have right now is getting in on this business, becoming an expert, and carving out your place *before* it becomes federally legal. If Prohibition had never been lifted, Kennedy might not have actually made as much money as he did. It will be your position when marijuana goes federally legal that will allow you to capitalize on a new level.

ONE BOURBON, ONE SCOTCH, ONE BEER

JOHN LEE HOOKER

Similarities in Marijuana and Alcohol

INTERESTINGLY, IT IS NOT ONLY TRUE that the marijuana industry resembles that of the alcohol industry during Prohibition, but also that marijuana and alcohol offer similar effects that humans crave – speaking to the growing marijuana market and customer base. I once saw the cover of a *National Geographic* magazine entitled, "Our 9,000-Year Love Affair With Booze." The author stated that "Alcohol isn't just a mind-altering drink: It has been a prime mover of human culture from the beginning, fueling the development of arts, language, and religion." All over the world, there are traditions involving alcohol. "In China, traditionally people toast at their weddings with rice wine that has been consumed for at least 9,000 years. In South America, the corn beer known as chicha has been a staple for thousands of years. France started making wine in earnest only after it was conquered by the Romans (as did most of Europe) and has never looked back."

The most interesting part of this story is that every country, tribe, and village on earth has some relationship with alcohol. The author argues that our desire for the "satisfied glow" that the ethanol in alcohol creates may be evolutionary. "From our modern point of view, ethanol has one very compelling property: It makes us feel good. Ethanol helps release serotonin, dopamine, and endorphins in the brain, chemicals that make us happy and less anxious. To our fruit-eating primate ancestors swinging through the trees, however, the ethanol in rotting fruit would have had three other appealing characteristics. First, it has a strong, distinctive smell that makes the fruit easy to locate. Second, it's easier to digest, allowing animals to get more of a commodity that was precious back then: calories. Third, its antiseptic qualities repel microbes that might sicken a primate. Millions of years ago, one of them developed a taste for fruit that had fallen from the tree ... We're pre-adapted for consuming alcohol."

We have since, as a race, found other ways to generate the desirable satisfied glow. This motivator drives the recreational market. Marijuana, like a measured amount of alcohol, can give people the ability to get buzzed, but not drunk. I mean, think about a time you had friends and family around, maybe a barbecue, warm weather, slight breeze, day off the next day. Alcohol lowers inhibitions, and that, in the most positive sense, can bring us closer together. That same satisfied glow can bring relief to medicinal marijuana patients, or simply relieve them of their pain.

We have evolved to seek the effects of these substances, and marijuana – unlike alcohol – is actually proving to be highly useful and beneficial to people's health and pain management. Marijuana is slowly becoming more acceptable to the general population because most people know it is relatively harmless for recreational use, and beneficial for medical use. Things have come a long way since the movie *Reefer Madness* (where marijuana was portrayed as being as bad as mustard gas). According to Fox News – we're talking conservative Fox News – nationally, 61 percent of people believe marijuana should be legalized, and only 33 percent do not believe it should be. The writing is on the wall as the scales continue to tip.

SMOKE TWO JOINTS

SUBLIME

Marijuana Over Alcohol and Opioids

UNLIKE THE ALCOHOL INDUSTRY DURING PROHIBITION, the marijuana industry is actually fighting to gain ground to offer a product that is much better for people than alcohol. While alcohol is enjoyable, it has very few documented positive effects, and many documented negative effects (both physical and social). As we talked about in *Get Real*, Americans are seeking ways to ease their pain – physical, mental, and situational – and many are turning to alcohol and opioids for relief. While I wish we lived in a society that could convince people to face and address the root causes of their pain differently, at least this industry is creating a market that allows people to engage with a healthier solution.

GET EDUCATED — THE OPPORTUNITY

ALCOHOL

In an article from Erin Brodwin, a biotech reporter for *Business Insider*, she reports that a scientific look at the harmful effects of alcohol versus marijuana resulted in "a clear answer" when it came to which was worse for you. The answer: alcohol is worse. Here are a few facts that she shares:

- In 2014, 30,722 people died from alcohol-induced causes in the US – and that does not count drinking-related accidents or homicides. If those deaths were included, the number would be closer to 90,000, according to the Centers for Disease Control and Prevention. Meanwhile, no deaths from marijuana overdoses have been reported, according to the Drug Enforcement Administration.

- For a 1994 survey, epidemiologists at the National Institute on Drug Abuse asked more than 8,000 people from ages fifteen to sixty-four about their drug use. Of those who had tried marijuana at least once, roughly 9 percent eventually fit a diagnosis of addiction. For alcohol, the figure was about 15 percent. To put that in perspective, the addiction rate for cocaine was 17 percent, while heroin was 23 percent, and nicotine was 32 percent.

- In November 2017, a group of the nation's top cancer doctors issued a statement asking people to drink less. They cited strong evidence that drinking alcohol – as little as a glass of wine or beer a day – increases the risk of developing both pre- and postmenopausal breast cancer. The US Department of Health lists alcohol as a known human carcinogen. Research highlighted by the National Cancer Institute suggests that the more alcohol you drink – particularly the more you drink regularly – the higher your risk of developing cancer. For marijuana, some research initially suggested a link between smoking and lung cancer, but that has been debunked. The report found that cannabis was not connected to an increased risk of lung cancers or head and neck cancers tied to smoking cigarettes.

- According to the National Council on Alcoholism and Drug Dependence, alcohol is a factor in 40 percent of all violent crimes, and a study of college students found that the rates of mental and physical abuse were higher on days when couples drank. On the other hand, no such relationship appears to exist for cannabis. A recent study looking at cannabis use and intimate partner violence in the first decade of marriage found that marijuana users were significantly less likely to commit violence against a partner than those who did not use the drug.

OPIOIDS

Crisis, anyone? America is in real trouble when it comes to opioid addiction, and what's so sad to me is that many of the people addicted to opioids began by taking them as prescriptions from doctors for legitimate pain. CBS News put out an article titled, "Drug Overdoses Killed More Americans Last Year Than the Vietnam War." It stated, "The latest numbers from the Centers for Disease Control and Prevention show that 64,070 people died from drug overdoses in 2016. That's a 21-percent increase over the year before. Approximately three-fourths of all drug overdose deaths are now caused by opioids – a class of drugs that includes prescription painkillers as well as heroin and potent synthetic versions like fentanyl." This statistic was then compared to other causes of death in recent years, and outstripped them all. The toll was greater than:

- The 35,092 motor vehicle deaths in 2015.

- AIDS-related deaths in the worst year of the AIDS crisis, when 50,628 people died in 1995.

- The peak year for homicides in the US, when 24,703 people were murdered in 1991.

- Suicides, which have been rising in the US for nearly 30 years and totaled 44,193 in 2015.

Can marijuana help reduce the deaths and addiction related to this crisis? Yes. Mainstream media continues to pick up on the new understanding of marijuana and share those understandings with the greater world. *The Washington Post* reported on two studies that specifically showed how marijuana could help the opioid crisis. The article shares that "Two studies published in the journal *JAMA Internal Medicine* find that the availability of medical and recreational marijuana is linked to lower rates of opiate prescribing. ... There is widespread agreement among doctors and public-health experts that marijuana is *effective in treating chronic pain. Doctors often treat that condition with opiate medication, despite little evidence that opiates* are effective for it. 'Marijuana is one of the potential alternative drugs that can provide relief from pain at a relatively lower risk of addiction and virtually no risk of overdose. ... These findings suggest that medical and adult-use marijuana laws have the potential to reduce opioid prescribing for Medicaid enrollees, a segment of the population with disproportionately high risk for chronic pain, opioid use disorder, and opioid overdose.'"

Ultimately, the marijuana industry, in response to the risks related to alcohol and opioids, has a chance to capitalize on a population of users currently turning to other substances, and capture those new users in the market that would actually support their health and well-being while also being beneficial financially to those in the industry. It's a win-win.

You may have heard there is a whole group of men over forty who are capable of working full-time and have just given up, they aren't even looking, they have just quit. Not having hope for the future and not fitting in can crush your spirit and ruin your life. This is why many people use alcohol and opioids dangerously. I believe the opportunities in this industry can restore hope. If you know people in that situation, get them this book. I can provide the tools and systems to turn things around if they are willing to change their viewpoint.

GOT TO GET YOU INTO MY LIFE

THE BEATLES

Marijuana's Health Benefits

JOHN LENNON SAID THIS SONG WAS PAUL MCCARTNEY'S ode to marijuana, so let's talk a bit more about the health benefits of marijuana, since you will need to be very clear about them in order to best know and serve marijuana-industry customers, as well as to address the naysayers who question why you're getting into this field. Kevin Loria, writing for *Business Insider*, combined the findings from many studies and reported on twenty-three documented health benefits of marijuana:

- It can treat glaucoma.
- It can help control epileptic seizures.
- A chemical found in marijuana stops cancer from spreading.

- It can decrease anxiety.
- THC slows the progression of Alzheimer's disease.
- It eases the pain of multiple sclerosis.
- It helps muscle spasms.
- It lessens the side effects of treating hepatitis C and increases treatment effectiveness.
- It treats inflammatory bowel diseases.
- It relieves arthritis pain.
- It helps keep your metabolism healthier.
- It improves symptoms of lupus.
- It improves creativity.
- It helps with Crohn's disease.
- It treats tremors for people with Parkinson's disease.
- It helps people suffering from PTSD.
- It protects the brain after a stroke.
- It might protect the brain from concussions and trauma.
- It can help eliminate nightmares.
- It reduces pain and nausea from chemo and stimulates the appetite of cancer patients.
- It may reverse the effects of tobacco and improve lung health.
- It decreases the symptoms of a severe seizure disorder known as Dravet syndrome.
- Users tend to be less obese and have a better response to eating sugar.

People continue to find ways to apply and use marijuana beneficially. It has even entered the veterinary world. Writer Alicia Antonio shared a personal story on mamamia.com about her fifteen-year-old cat who was saved through the use of CBD oil.

Her cat Charli came down with a neurological problem (likely a brain tumor) that she didn't have the money to get diagnosed and treated. The vet had recommended putting the cat down, but she couldn't bring herself to do it.

Her grandmother had been encouraged to use CBD oil to shrink a brain tumor, with some success, and so she looked into trying it with her cat. CBD oil doesn't get users high. It is purely for therapeutic benefit, without the harsh side effects that you typically find with prescribed pharmaceutical drugs. Alicia wrote, "Within four days of starting on CBD oil twice a day, Charli started to eat and drink on her own again. Prior to that, she had been refusing all food and water and I had to keep her hydrated (and alive) by using a baby syringe to get water down her throat. Five days after starting on the CBD oil, she was able to use her front legs again and was able to slowly sit up and prop herself up against walls and furniture, even though her back legs still did not work. The following day, her back legs started to work again, but she was weak and wobbly and struggled to take more than a few steps. A full week after starting on CBD oil, our cat was up and walking again – albeit tentatively. A month on, and Charli is 95 percent her previous self. She shows no real signs of any illness. She can jump up on chairs again. Her appetite and toileting habits are back to normal. Her head tic is gone. Her pupils are back to normal. Because I've had her for so long, I can see that she doesn't walk quite as well as she once did, but most people wouldn't know otherwise. She has resumed her life of luxury and spends her days sunning herself in the window, or lounging on the couch." (You may want to check out Alicia's full story. She also references her friend with multiple sclerosis who used medicinal marijuana to successfully relieve pain.)

Ultimately, the benefits of marijuana are monumental to individuals and their families. In my personal experience, I was dating a woman whose father had cancer, and we helped with the caregiving, each taking a few days of the week to assist. I say this cautiously, but it was a wonderful and rewarding experience. Obviously, it was terrible he was dying, but it was also a gift to provide real love and care when he was facing his worst situation. The marijuana I provided was in the form of ice cream and brownies. This particular person was fairly conservative by nature and was not excited about the idea of trying it. However, when someone is in that position, they see the positive in having an alternative to what had already been tried. His nausea was difficult to deal with, and this was something that helped. If you know someone who is, or was, struggling with the end-of-life stages, you know what I mean. With so many emotions and so much physical pain, not to mention wondering about what's next and lingering on potential regrets, having hope of some relief is an extraordinary benefit.

PREDICTION

STEEL PULSE

What's Ahead in this Industry?

HERE IS MY PREDICTION FOR THE FUTURE of the marijuana industry:

- The federal government will remove marijuana from a Class 1 distinction. Marijuana will be legal nationwide in America and Europe (and hopefully China) with a distinction between medical and recreational.

- The majority of marijuana will be commoditized, while there will still be a market for specialty and niche brands.

- Medical research will confirm marijuana's many health benefits.

- Marijuana will surpass opiates as the main pain prescription.

- Smokable marijuana will be increasingly rare.

- There will be custom-made synthetic strains that can treat individual health conditions.

- Technology, like the use of apps, in particular, will be embraced in this field as tools that create better, more interactive relationships with customers.

- The stigma will be removed from this product and related industries, and it will be as common as a great glass of wine.

- Pharmaceutical companies will be actively involved in its development, and food, alcohol, tobacco, and even makeup companies will engage in the recreational side.

- Vapes, edibles, and some smoking products will be sold in major stores as well as boutique stores (Starbucks and mom and pop stores).

- The banking industry will treat this industry like any other business, free of the current restrictions and hurdles.

MY LIFE

BILLY JOEL

Battling Naysayers

NOW, I'M NOT SAYING THAT THIS INDUSTRY is all roses and sunshine. It can be tough. What you will find is that people have strong opinions about this movement. If you enter into this field, some of the things you'll hear from family and friends could be:

- It's a Class 1 registered drug; what are you thinking?

- This is federally illegal; do you want to lose all your money?

- Who's to say that if you invest all this time, money, and energy, you will ever get a return?

- The rules change every five minutes; how do you know what you're doing today will be relevant tomorrow?

- You know you can't use a bank to deposit money? (Not true.) That should tell you something.

- Do you really want to contribute to young people getting stoned?

I hope that you could now tackle some of these questions, given all the information you now have about this opportunity. But just in case, let's address these one by one.

CONCERN: IT'S A CLASS 1 REGISTERED DRUG

A: This is true, AND this is why the time to take action is now. The fact that this is true keeps out every public company, and almost everyone who is a "rule follower," so in other words, most good businesspeople. You have a once-in-a-lifetime chance to position yourself in the market before the big guys (publicly traded companies) can get in.

CONCERN: IT IS FEDERALLY ILLEGAL

A: True again. Can you lose all your money? Technically, yes. But in states where voters have approved it, IF you are following all the laws as enacted, you will be fine. The state of Colorado has a Marijuana Enforcement Department. THAT is the state government, and it makes a great argument if you were ever to run into federal trouble.

CONCERN: INVESTING TIME, MONEY, AND ENERGY WITH NO GUARANTEE

A: This is not a simple business. If you want that, go buy a Subway franchise or something simple. However, then you'll never have the chance to make it big and pave your own way. People in Colorado and other states are making huge money. To quote a line from *Scarface*, "Your biggest problem ... is what to do with all the fucking cash!"

CONCERN: RULES CHANGE QUICKLY

A: True, but there is time to change and adapt with them. There is a reasonableness to this, and the state government knows that things change quickly.

CONCERN: YOU CANNOT USE A BANK SINCE IT IS CONSIDERED "DRUG MONEY"

A: Partially true, for now. It will change for the better. What you can do now is use an app to purchase cannabis without cash, and there is also a provision where you can "get banked," meaning that you can have your cash deposited in a federal bank. It's done like this: the bank has to make sure you are compliant with state marijuana laws, just like another set of eyes on the business. They charge anywhere from $1,200 to $1,500 per month, and then you can use their bank.

CONCERN: YOU WILL BE CONTRIBUTING TO THE RISK OF YOUNG PEOPLE TAKING DRUGS

A: In a recent article from FOX News, in the states where marijuana is legal, the number of young people using marijuana has declined. Colorado is seen as the beacon, and the state's process is being duplicated in other states because we've had success doing this the right way, with extraordinary results.

Remember, you are now grounded in your why – your legacy, your big dreams, your declaration, and your goals. Naysayers will be a bump in the road. Decide now that no one can talk you down.

GET IT DONE

YOUNG AMERICANS

DAVID BOWIE

We Are Underdogs

AMERICANS LOVE THE UPSET, DON'T WE? It is easiest to see in sports. If we were talking sports and I said, "1980," most people would think about the US men's hockey team beating the Russians in the Winter Olympic Games. The Russian team had been playing together for a decade and hadn't lost a game in as many years. The Americans were a team of college kids who had played together for six months. The match was a seemingly impossible feat for the Americans before they could compete for the gold medal against Sweden. If I said, "Hitler's Olympics," most people would think about Jesse Owens. You know the history of Hitler trying to manufacture the "Master Aryan Race" and then displaying it to the world at the Nazi-hosted event. Backfire. Owens won four gold medals, while Hitler steamed, watching from the stands. Other beloved upsets? Muhammad Ali beat George Foreman in the Rumble in the Jungle, the Jets beat the Colts in the 1969 Super Bowl, and NC State won the national championship in 1983 against Houston's "Phi Slama Jama." Just recently, the Philadelphia Eagles won the Super Bowl by beating one of the greatest teams in NFL history, the New England Patriots, who many believe have the greatest quarterback and the greatest coach of all time. The Eagles won with a backup quarterback and a second-year coach.

We like upsets in movies, too: *Scarface* (until the end), *The Killing Fields*, all the *Rocky* movies, *The Karate Kid movies*, *Remember the Titans*, *Erin Brockovich*, *Silver Linings Playbook*, *The Pursuit of Happyness*, and *Tin Cup*, to name a few. In all of these upsets – sports and movies – causing the upset required hard work and persistence. On paper, none of these upsets should have happened. If you've seen *Tin Cup*, this book is not about laying up (one of my favorite scenes ever). If it takes a twelve on the final hole, so be it. No one can guarantee results, but you can guarantee how you play.

These stories are exciting and inspiring, which is why they feel good to us. We love the underdog story. The main reason we love the underdog story is that it is a part of our DNA as Americans. The key story of America and how it was formed lies in the colonies and their victory in the Revolutionary War.

I believe that America becoming an independent nation and fighting against Great Britain is the greatest upset in the history of the world.

Let's look at it on paper:

THE THIRTEEN COLONIES	GREAT BRITAIN
• No country formed • No established currency • Struggling to build an economy • No traditional military • Limited naval presence	• One of the world's strongest countries • One of the oldest established currencies • One of the strongest economies in the world • Strong military with additional hired mercenaries • The strongest naval force in the world

On paper, you'd think there would be no way to win the Revolutionary War. What we know, however, is that logic, numbers, and formulas don't tell the size of the heart; the power of commitment; or the belief in one's own, or a collective, destiny. So why did the US win our independence in this unlikely matchup?

We had a bold plan and the courage to pursue it at all costs. By issuing the Declaration of Independence, adopted by the Continental Congress on July 4, 1776, the thirteen American colonies severed their political connections to Great Britain. The Declaration summarized the colonists' motivations for seeking independence. While the quest for independence was obviously difficult and complex, I believe the colonists took the same steps I am going to ask you to make when you create your declaration in our last Get It Done section:

- They made a Declaration: they declared independence from British rule.

- They Formulated "unreasonable" goals: their ambitious goals were unhampered by their reality because they believed the goals were possible.

- They had a Deadline: they used the signing of the declaration to force their own hand as well as England's. There was no going back.

- They had the Integrity to fight for something greater than themselves.

- They defined the Pathway to success with a plan.

- They Insisted that their cause was righteous.

- They Took Control of the war: even when control meant dragging out the war and using "unorthodox" tactics for the time, they did it.

And to be totally fair, without help from France, we probably wouldn't have won.

All of these steps took strength and resolve of character – it is our nation's legacy. Americans during the Revolutionary War didn't look outside themselves for an answer to their aspirations; they leveraged who they were and what they had to make a change. If you're American, then you are born to be an underdog and to face the odds. That's why you are drawn to entrepreneurship. That's why, faced with a massive, untapped opportunity, you are considering getting on the battlefield and making your stand. You may not see yourself as an underdog, but if you are reading this to launch a better future, then it's you against your current reality and roadblocks. If you do see yourself as an underdog, then you're in the perfect place, 'cause I'm one too, and it's our time to win.

KING

UB40

Martin Luther King Jr.

I KNOW THAT RANDOM SHOOTINGS ARE ON THE RISE, and it's a cause of anxiety for Americans, but what if you were at work and got the news that someone had bombed your family's house where your spouse and ten-week-old child were?

Honestly, think about it for a moment. How would you feel? What would you do? Feel enraged? Fight back? Seek revenge? It's complicated, right? When it happened to Dr. Martin Luther King Jr, here is what happened …

From an article on Sunday, January 29, 2012, by Michael Buchanan on ReasonableDoubt.org:

On January 30, 1956, King was speaking at a meeting that

had been organized to support the bus boycott. While at that meeting, some person or persons planted an explosive device on the front porch of King's residence. The bomb exploded, blowing out the windows of the house and causing significant damage to the front porch of the family home.

During the meeting, King heard about the explosion at his residence and was told that his wife and child had not been injured. King told the crowd what had happened and quickly left. Nearing his home, King saw a crowd of black men, some brandishing guns and knives, and a multitude of white policemen around his residence. King rushed inside, pushing through the crowd in his home to the back room, making sure that his wife, Coretta, and ten-week-old daughter had not been injured.

When King returned to the front room of the house, some white journalists were trying to leave to file their reports, but could not get out of the house, which was surrounded by armed, angry supporters of Martin Luther King Jr. King walked out onto his damaged front porch and held up his hand for silence. King spoke in a calm and peaceful voice, telling the crowd that everything was all right and that no one had been injured. King spoke to the crowd as follows:

> *'Don't get panicky. Don't do anything panicky. Don't get your weapons. If you have weapons, take them home. He who lives by the sword will perish by the sword. Remember that is what Jesus said. We are not advocating violence. We want to love our enemies. I want you to love our enemies. Be good to them. This is what we must live*

by. We must meet hate with love.

I did not start this boycott. I was asked by you to serve as your spokesman. I want it to be known the length and breadth of this land that if I am stopped, this movement will not stop. If I am stopped, our work will not stop. For what we are doing is right. What we are doing is just. And God is with us.

Upon hearing these words, King's supporters were calmed and eventually left the area peaceably. King's calmness and peaceful demeanor impressed many of the city officials, police and reporters that were gathered at the scene of the bombing."

Martin Luther King Jr. was one of the most transformative Americans. He was obviously a brilliant speaker, but if you look up some of his interviews, he was even more impressive "off the cuff." (See YouTube for the Mike Wallace show, in three parts. Exceptional.)

To me, his greatest strength was his commitment to his mission and vision. He never wavered, even under the immense pressure for him to change or go away or alter his position. I've coined the term "supra-circumstantial." It's not a real word, but the combination of a few:

Supra means above, especially when referring to parts of a text, above it, above circumstances.

Circumstances means a condition, detail, part, or attribute, with respect to time, place, manner, agent, etc., that accompanies, determines, or modifies a fact or event, a modifying or influencing factor.

King had a vision for black people to be treated as equals.

Nothing else would be acceptable. He was also aware enough to know that white people wouldn't treat black people as equals yet, but his job was to have white people see black people as human beings first, then we could get to equality. What he endured and what so many others endured, especially in the South, is a national tragedy, but King tackled the tragedy by being supra-circumstantial.

What does this have to do with you and your business? Simple. What if we were supra-circumstantial about our lives and our businesses? What could we accomplish if we are committed to our righteous outcomes, no matter what the circumstances? We have things so much easier in many ways than many others before us. I want you to adopt this concept for your life, and with all the tools, systems, and procedures put forth in this book, anything is possible. Right?

HERE COMES THE SUN

THE BEATLES

Generate Positive Personal Energy

MY SON ASKED ME A QUESTION THE OTHER DAY that stumped me for a few minutes. It was such a simple question. It was a cloudy day, and he asked, "Where is the sun?" I simply replied, "It's there, we just can't see it right now." But I wasn't positive why. How could the sun, as powerful as it is, be stopped by something that hardly exists? You probably know already, but it's simply because the beams of light are being scattered. It's just like water being run through a filter; the clouds are the filter that diffuses the power and scatters the energy.

The sun burns 600 million tons of fuel every second and produces 400 trillion watts of energy per second. This is the equivalent to detonating a trillion-megaton nuclear bomb every second. We, of course, depend on the sun for almost every aspect of life on Earth. We take it for granted because it is always just there, like the air.

It got me thinking: what if you and I are like the sun? Meaning, what if we are the generators of the most powerful and life-affirming energy, the anchors of our own solar systems of relationships? Some people will never be out of our orbit, some will drift past us like asteroids, and some people will zoom by us like comets – and we can have a positive effect on all of them.

The point is, every day, we have the opportunity to generate positive energy with every person we encounter. You've heard the saying, "That person walks in a room and it lights up." Don't just light up the room, CHANGE THE TEMPERATURE. Melt the clouds of negative judgments, thoughts, and feelings that can temporarily scatter your energy, but never diminish your true force.

MIND POWER

MIND POWER

Making Your Declaration

YOU'VE TAKEN THE TIME TO *Get Real*, *Get Clear*, and *Get Educated*. In order to "*Get It Done*," we're going to put a stamp on these first three steps by creating a personal declaration that will sustain you in your work – and help you remain supra-circumstantial. This declaration must become your mantra, something you say to yourself every day, at least once in the morning and once before you go to sleep. Soon you will have it memorized, and you will wake up thinking it and being it. This declaration is the "placebo" pill[1]

---

[1] *The Placebo Effect is a beneficial effect, produced by a placebo drug or treatment that CANNOT be attributed to the properties of the placebo itself, and MUST therefore be due to the patient's BELIEF in that treatment. Scientists have proven that our brains' belief in something can cause actual physical changes in us. It is called "expectancy theory" – what the brain believes about the immediate future.*

your mind needs to take so that your affirmation and vision get rehearsed in your head and become a reality. Remember, what you think about yourself, what you expect from yourself, your viewpoint, and what you expect from the world around you matters significantly to your actual results. As an inspiration to invest in this process, to invest in the power of your brain, here is a story about how a man responded to a placebo medication – thinking it was real – and what happened when he heard the truth.

Sandra Blakeslee from the New York Times *wrote an article entitled, "Placebos Prove So Powerful Even Experts Are Surprised; New Studies Explore the Brain's Triumph Over Reality." Her article centered on the story of Mr. Wright. She writes, "Many doctors know the story of "Mr. Wright," who was found to have cancer in 1957, and was given only days to live. Hospitalized in Long Beach, California, with tumors the size of oranges, he heard that scientists had discovered a horse serum, Krebiozen, that appeared to be effective against cancer. He begged to receive it. His physician, Dr. Philip West, finally agreed and gave Mr. Wright an injection on a Friday afternoon. The following Monday, the astonished doctor found his patient out of his 'death bed,' joking with the nurses. The tumors, the doctor wrote later, 'had melted like snowballs on a hot stove.' Two months later, Mr. Wright read medical reports that the horse serum was a quack remedy. He suffered an immediate relapse. 'Don't believe what you read in the papers,' the doctor told Mr. Wright. Then he injected him with what he said was, 'a new super-refined double strength' version of the drug. Actually, it was water, but again, the tumor masses melted. Mr. Wright was 'the picture of health' for another two months – until he read a definitive report stating that Krebiozen was worthless. He died two days later."*

You control the truth your brain accepts, and what it then anticipates about the future. Use its power to transform your outcome. For many of you, entering into this field is flipping a new page in your personal story. For all of you, I hope this book makes you flip the way you think about yourself and approach your goals. Remember the acronym, I FLIP IT, as you go on this journey. Remember, the most important part of the American story is the Declaration of Independence. You'll note the framers didn't start with: "When we're a fully complete nation, we will (circumstance) … when everyone else in the world agrees, we will (circumstance) … when we have the strongest military, we will (circumstance) …The new United States declared on July 4, 1776, that Great Britain will no longer rule us and we are free to create a government of the people, by the people, for the people.

I DECLARE

List the affirmations that are the flip of your mental obstacles (refer back to the *Sound And Vision* chapter in *Get Real*), the things that you want to be sure direct your work every day.

- Remember, when you declare something, it is real right now.
- Be bold.

FORMULATE

Choose your goals and name your WHY (think about your legacy and your impact).

- Keep in mind, you choose these goals for a reason, but that is different than being reasonable when you imagine what you can do. Being "reasonable" in the traditional sense often is what holds us back. Be unreasonable, and know your why.
- Think big.
- Make your goals SMART.

LINE IN THE SAND

Give yourself a deadline (three months, five years …) or deadlines (for steps in the process).

INTEGRITY

Know your values and stick to them.

PATHWAY

Name your plan to get where you want to go.

- Make a roadmap of where you want to go. Write down what you will need to do and what it will take to get there.

INSIST

Be persistent in pursuing what you want, in spite of difficulties.

TAKE CONTROL

Have the discipline to know yourself and be in control of your thoughts, emotions, and decisions. Choose to be supra-circumstantial.

Your declaration will be made up of the first I and F in the acronym … I Declare, and Formulate (IF!). Here is mine:

I DECLARE:
I love people.
I see the best in myself and others.
I have all the tools I need.
I always keep going.
The more successful I am, the more others will benefit.
I always make a positive difference.
Everything works out the way I want it to.
When obstacles show up, I smile at them like an old friend.

(F:) I will change the lives and fortunes of at least one million people in America and the World, through my book, seminars, tools, and coaching, within three years.

We all have negative thoughts that come up, just like negative judgments about things and people. If we let those thoughts rule us, we are working against ourselves. Your daily declaration will help you battle these thoughts away. Next, make a list of the great things you already own and have accomplished; this will remind you of how much you have already won. Lastly, if you have a partner who is totally with you on this, make an agreement with them to be supportive. If not, I have a plan for you. You may know that we are more likely to let ourselves down than to let another person down. If you made an agreement to meet with a friend to work out at 5:00 a.m. and you know they will be there, you will very likely go. If you have an agreement with yourself to go workout by yourself at 5:00 a.m., that bed feels warm on a cold day, and you might have trouble. Make and sign a contract with yourself, listing out what you are going to do and what the consequences are if you don't make your own agreements.

Our number-one driver as humans, at the most basic level, is to survive, and our brains make thousands of judgments in milliseconds all the time to protect us. The other night, I was walking into a grocery store, and a man was standing there with a dog on a leash. I always have good connections with animals, and as I walked up, I was expecting to pet this dog for a moment before going on. I find that taking an interest in people's pets helps me connect with people in the moment. It was dark, and this dog turned and looked at me as I approached. It didn't wag its tail or give any welcoming indications. In a moment, I went from, "This will be sweet, I'll pet this dog," to, "This dog might bite me." The man standing there made no move and didn't say anything, so I walked out a little farther and just decided to skip it. Why? Because I didn't want to potentially spook the dog as I was walking into the light from the dark, and get bitten. This is not some great moment in human development, but it is one of a thousand instances that happen every day, often subconsciously.

Unfortunately, this also means that our base instincts to "stay safe" and "be reasonable" keep us from taking the unreasonable risks that can have the greatest reward. Your declaration should give you regular motivation and confidence to keep pursuing your big dreams and fight any instincts that make you hold something back because you are afraid of the risk.

Go. All. In.

Write your personal declaration (your IF) here, and start saying it at least twice every day:

_____

_____

_____

_____

_____

_____

_____

_____

_____

_____

_____

_____

_____

_____

_____

_____

_____

_____

_____

_____

_____

LET MY LOVE OPEN THE DOOR

PETE TOWNSEND

My Dad and My Own Revolution

A FEW PEOPLE SUGGESTED THAT I LEAVE THIS CHAPTER out of the book, but I chose to include it anyway. I will tell you why at the end, but by then, hopefully, it will be clear to you.

If your parents divorced when you were young, hopefully it was better for you than it was for me. It was uncomfortable, unpleasant, confusing, disappointing, straight-up painful, and difficult. I was thirteen, and for my brother and me, as you might remember, it had the added wrinkle that we had moved with our mom from Virginia to California as a result of the divorce.

My dad remained in Virginia as the CFO of Martin Marietta Aluminum, headquartered in Bethesda, Maryland. After we moved, I only saw him a few times in those next years. Part of the problem was that my dad was a WWII veteran, and if you know any of those guys, they usually think emotions should be buried and covered with smoking, drinking, and hard work. The Greatest Generation got a ton done to avoid dealing with their real pain. Obviously, significant trade-offs.

My dad essentially gave up on having any relationship with my brother and me after a nasty and hard-fought divorce from our mom and stopped communicating with us completely. Now that I can look back, it makes sense knowing the lack of tools he had available personally.

A few years after graduating from high school, my brother and I were in Southern California, and we knew my dad had retired in Palm Desert about three hours away. I hadn't seen him in at least five years and didn't expect to when out of nowhere we got a call from the woman he had married. She said, "Your dad has cancer and you boys should come out to see him and say goodbye." Of course, we were shocked and saddened and chose to go. The next day, we grabbed dress clothes, hung them in the back of the car, and set out. We talked a lot on the way out and were filled with nervous energy and unease.

When we got to his eighteen-hole golf course community, we pulled in down the street, changed into our nice clothes, and drove to the guard gate. I said hello and asked to see Mr. Robin Johnson. The guard called, and then came back and said, "He says, 'no visitors.'" I said, "Yeah, but does he know it's his sons?" The guard said, "Yes, he doesn't want to let you in."

In that moment, you could have knocked me over. I just couldn't believe it. I said to my brother, "Fuck that guy," and that was it for me.

Over the next ten years, we weren't in contact at all. I didn't expect things to change and got used to it (while I was pretending that it didn't bother me).

After working many odd jobs through college and graduating with a political science degree and a minor in philosophy, I saved up some money to start a business with a lifelong friend in Colorado. My friend had already registered the name and found a store location.

My friend's fiancé had gone through a personal development seminar, and we got into a discussion about relationships. She said that if I didn't look at my father as being a jerk, he wouldn't be one. I said, "But he is one, can't you see that?" She said my viewpoint about my father determined what he was to me. I thought about it for a long time, and the more I thought about it, the more it made sense. It was a revolutionary moment for me. It gave me back control over my life instead of being a victim of circumstance. Even though it was twenty years ago this year, I remember where I was when we discussed it, and my life has never been the same since.

There are stories, and there are facts. There are very few actual facts in the world. My dad and I had not spoken or seen each other in a long time – fact. All the emotion, pain, judgment, disappointment, blaming, and complaining – story. The story is more powerful emotionally than the facts, and that is what drives us, sometimes, to the wrong choices. My friend's fiancé was pushing me to find a story that had us both win.

I was inspired by my friend to reach out to my dad to see what could be salvaged. But this time, I had a new strength, a new resolve, and I had a new story.

Facts: My dad was born in 1923 in the poor Tennessee south, to a mainly uneducated family. His mother died when he was twelve, and his father moved from relationship to relationship. He was forced to sleep in the entryway of the house and was beaten regularly. His sister says he was beaten so severely, his legs stuck to the sheets. He worked three jobs to put himself through the University of Tennessee, where he earned a finance degree and was president of his fraternity. He dropped all contact with his father and moved up through the world after serving in WWII.

Story: My dad had a rough time growing up and didn't have a role model to see what a good father was. He also grew up in a time when men speaking about their feelings and dealing with emotions was not "natural." He believed in his heart that he was doing a great job for my mom, my brother, and me. He was blind-sided by the divorce and was in such pain he didn't adequately know how to deal with it or rectify the situation. He felt he had to shut down to survive, so he shut my brother and me out.

Now, can you see how that changes everything? This is a story that has us both win. He never said these things to me, but it probably wasn't far off, and it doesn't matter. Because changing the story gives humanity to everyone, and it allowed me to lead from a place of sympathy and caring rather than judgment.

I took this newly created story and put it to the test immediately. I called him out of the blue to see what could be done. I remember sitting at a desk downstairs, finding the number, and dialing his landline phone.

I heard it ringing. I was very nervous.

"Hello?"

"Hey dad, this is your son, Todd Johnson."

"Uh, um, I think you have the wrong number."

And he hung up.

I was totally stunned. And then I got angry.

I have to admit, I went right back to being mad at myself for putting myself out there again. But about ten minutes later, after processing it and dealing with it a little, I had the funniest feeling. I chuckled out loud when I realized that my dad didn't know who I was at all. And if he thought that he was going to stop me by hanging up, he had another thing coming. So I waited a week and called again, and this time a woman answered and told me not to call anymore. I said, "Thanks for the advice, but until I hear it from him, I won't stop."

I called after another week, and he answered and promptly hung up again. I smiled and said to myself, "Okay, no problem. I'll get you sooner or later."

Then I broke through about three weeks after I initially called, and we spoke.

I remember it like it was yesterday. He said, "What do you want?"

"Dad, I'm calling to apologize (you could have heard a pin drop). I have been blaming you for us not being in touch all these years, and I recently realized that I haven't done anything to work this out with you. I have been waiting for you and not doing anything myself. I want to let you know that you did do a lot of great things for us as children, and I have never thanked you for them. As an adult with responsibilities, I understand more who you are and how much you did. I'm going to die someday and you're going to die someday. I want you to know that I love you and things are not going to continue the way they have been. I'm going to do what I need to do, reach out to you, see you when possible, send you birthday cards and Father's Day cards, and generally be a good son, and you can do what you have to do. If you want to call, great. If not, no problem. It's not going to interrupt things."

He said, "Ah, ah, okay." And that was that.

I was elated. It felt great to take charge of such a righteous mission and just plow through. It was a start.

Through the next few years, while I was in Colorado and he was in California, we spoke, but when I went out there to visit my mom, he always refused to see me. And after a few years, it became frustrating and I felt I needed to do something to break up the pattern.

I happened to be in Los Angeles for a week of training with a job. I found online directions to his home and drove there. For some reason, there was no street parking, so I had to park a mile away. I walked toward his house while wearing a dress shirt, slacks, and dress shoes. This was the summer in Palm Desert, probably about 120 degrees. Soaked with sweat when I arrived, I purposely skipped the guard station and headed to the side of the complex. My only option was to scale the eight-foot wall. I felt strange jumping into his neighborhood and walking around like a criminal.

I found his address and checked the mailbox to make sure the mail was his. I couldn't believe I was reading his name on his mail. It looked so familiar and yet unfamiliar. I walked across the street and stood in front of his security screen door that had such tiny holes in it that I couldn't see through. The heart-pounding moment had arrived. I knocked and waited anxiously. No answer. I was sweating so much that I wanted a retreat from the sun for just a few minutes, so I walked back across the street and stood under a tree, wondering how I could be so close yet not get through to him. I chose to give it one more knock. This time, I knocked hard. And the door opened, and from behind that screen door, I couldn't see him but …

I heard him say, "Hello, can I help you?"

"Yes, it's your son, Todd Johnson."

"You're kidding."

"No."

"Well, come on in."

He poured me a Coke with ice, and we sat in the kitchen. He started with, "How did you get in here?" I said, "I jumped the fence." He said, "Don't do that again." I said, "You let me in, and I won't." He said, "I will." We sipped our Cokes.

The spell had been broken. My dad was six-foot-four, 240 pounds, very intense and powerful. This was the first time I had ever seen him nervous. Once he knew I wasn't going to deliver the beat-down conversation that he was a bad father, he felt safe. When he felt safe, he opened up. When he opened up, we connected, and when we connected, love was present.

From then on, we spent time over the next three years (obviously he had made it through his earlier bout with cancer), at holidays and football games and the basic stuff, listening to Ray Charles, Sam Cooke, and Roger Miller. The amazing thing that happened along the way is that I honestly started out selfishly doing this for me. I didn't want to feel like I hadn't done my best, in case he did die, without cleaning this up. And what happened is that he became the father I had always wanted him to be. Not all the way, but it was amazing what could be generated with a commitment to something great, and having love and forgiveness be the guide.

One day, I got a call from my dad's doctor, who told me that he had advanced lung cancer and would likely pass in two weeks. My aunt and I got him to the recovery hospital and then home, and he started getting better.

My dad turned eighty on August 26, 2003, and since it was likely his last birthday, I got in touch with everyone he knew and thought he would enjoy hearing from. I asked everyone to include something special, a letter or a photo. I put together a book that included pictures of him through the years, with letters and pictures from friends. It closed with letters from my brother and me, and when he read the letters, he cried (which was no small miracle).

Todd and his Dad 2003

I stayed with him off and on for over three months out of the last six months he lived. It was difficult, but I wanted him to know more than anything that he had someone in his corner, no matter what. I got the groceries, made the meals, drove him to appointments, cleaned up, picked up, and made sure his oxygen line never got caught on anything. There were times when he was very weak, heavily medicated, and feeling his worst. He needed help with small things, but I knew he was a prideful guy. I said, "Dad, this is how it's supposed to work. You were there to help me when I needed it, and now I'm here to help you. I'm happy to be the one to do it." He replied, "I can't tell you how much it means to me."

The day after Thanksgiving, my brother was there visiting him, and it became clear that my father was close to the end. My brother called me in tears and told me I better get out there right away if I wanted to say goodbye. I went straight to the airport and got on the first flight available, then I rented a car and raced all the way from Orange County to Palm Springs. I ran to the front door and then to his room. At my dad's bedside, I held his hand, reminded him how much I loved him, thanked him for who he was, and told him he had done a great job. I left the room, and twenty minutes after I got there, he died. Although I can't prove it, I believe he had been waiting for me. Even though I was deeply sad, the situation couldn't have been any more complete.

As I said earlier: life is measured in moments. The moment you fall in love, the moment you graduate, the moment you find out you're having a baby, the moment your child is born, the moment the game is over and you won, the moment you know you want to be an entrepreneur, the moment you make the choice that things are going to be different. It's all about the moments that move us … that change our future forever.

I had justifiable reasons not to work things out with my dad, and they were reasonable. He was my dad, he should have known better, he should have been the one to make up with me, he should have apologized first, and on and on … but I chose to be unreasonable.

This feels difficult to explain, but I'm going to give it a shot because it is like a Teflon coating of power, and I want you to have it. I do not honor things that are not honorable. Meaning, when my dad hung up on me, I did get upset the first time, then realized that this was his "bark," his attempt to get me to bite on his fake "front" to leave him alone. His bark was really about him protecting himself, NOT rejecting me. So I ignored it; it wasn't really true, so I gave it no power or acknowledgment. Believe it or not, sometimes people will test you to see if you will bite and if you do, it might confirm their story in their head about you. I pressed on unfazed because the end goal was to have love, time, care, and enjoyment together, and I wasn't going to let some bullshit stop all that. I never let anyone take my power.

I included this deeply personal chapter to illustrate this point: it's difficult to be strong in your business life if you are weak in your personal life. Once I repaired my relationship with my dad, I felt this incredible energy of positive power to BE the difference and create the greatest outcomes in every area of my life, including my business. When your power is limited by problems, mistakes or regrets (amongst other things), you don't burn as bright, and as a result, you don't feel as free to move forward and make changes. For example, you're late to a meeting then feel uncomfortable engaging fully, or you are unfulfilled at your job but don't take the steps to leave. You stay in a personal relationship longer than you know you should. You're not getting what you want from it, but at least you're not alone. You get in an argument with a neighbor, so you avoid going past their house when you head out with your kids. None of these are as monumental as the history my dad and I overcame, but even these small areas of "not okay" in your life will hold you back.

Take a deep breath. Face them. Clean them up (here's how to clean something up: ask that person for a few uninterrupted minutes and work it out, yes, apologizing won't kill you). Plus, many people like to say, "That person really pushes my buttons." Ah, you don't have any buttons and neither does anyone else.

I hope you will think about your personal life, all of the

relationships you value or once valued, and make a choice to be the difference. Make a choice that things are going to be different in your life and in the lives of those you love, from now on.

Full power, full time.

THANK YOU
(FALETTINME BE MICE ELF AGIN)
SLY AND THE FAMILY STONE
Acknowledgments

I'VE BEEN LUCKY TO HAVE SUCH GREAT PEOPLE in my life since as far back as I can remember. To me, when you are around good people who know you well, it's a gift, and it allows you to be the best version of yourself.

Genuine acknowledgment is one of the most powerful tools we have to connect with each other and elevate one another. So, if you're on this list, you already know how I feel about you and what I appreciate about your contributions and our relationship because I've told you many times already (hey, you know, it's part of my charm). Thank you.

Miss G, Quinn McCoy, Calvin Marshall, The World Famous

Bubbles, Nadia Comaneci Bielous Johnson, The Sommerville Special: RFJ, Sun-In Stephen: SRJ, The Boss Candy, Dr. Vince, Meem, Dr. Generous G., Ulysses S. B., Sidney, Skye, Chewy Alex, Faconnable Tracy, Theo Alex, Michael G., Baba Grace, Steve, Marie, George, Lois, Richard, Christine, Kathy, Kay, Keep on Truckin' Jim, Trevis, Donalyn, Doaker, Always a Flyer: Uncle Dick, Nellie Bligh, Beth, Cap, Justin Caruso, All of the Jennifer Dulles Family, Bruce Granger, Jason Jansky, Bob Kite, Miss Ashley, Marquez, Leslie Reed, Charles Murphy and Christy, Craig and Kath McDonald, Phil Nearing, Megan O'Brien, Michael Campsie, Bojan Kalajdzic, Reid Wegler, Reba R., Jennifer Jas, Holly Silber, Steve Sandier, Don Schneider, Christopher Johnson, Michael Collins, Eric Scott, Willie Scott, Randy Owens, Robert Skrzynski, Darren Milner, Lewie Pettit, All of the Carlos Camerena Family, Steve Coleman, Mr. Kody Kay Kittley, Mallory Smith, Betty, Yohannes Kassa, Booker T. Walshe, Jimmy Reilly, Jimmy Bertha, Jimmy Koustas, Dan Morgan, Momida, Efren Corral, Miguel Angel Anaya Garcia, Aide, Connor Lavis, Kevin Green, Matt Hartinov, Reese Levin, Clifton and Geneva Jones, Shawn Clifton, Cameron Willingham, Debbie Kendall, Gary Bagby, Dick Stuetz, Dr. James McDonald, Dr. Michael Rich, Dr. Thomas Imhoff, Nancy T., John T., Heidel, Tom S., Josh James, Michael B., Nicole B., Joe A., Jeff K., Chris Raby, Bill Krause, Major Wood, Colette B., Nancy I., Laura E., Daniel-son, Becca Bloch and Steve, Melissa and Pete Livingston, Lindsey and Matt Armstrong, Pat Leach, Marc Leach, Chip Aker, Annie McDonald, Howard Hughes, David B., Syl S., Martin Luther King Jr., John F. Kennedy, Helen Keller, Charles Mingus, Ayrton Senna, Dr. Haing S. Ngor, Napoleon Hill, Vincent Bugliosi, Rod Serling, Frank F., Frank P., Kenny R., Jimmy, Rocky, Orson Welles and last, but certainly not least, E.A. Martin.

WHAT'S MY NAME (WHO AM I)

SNOOP DOGG

About the Author

TODD JOHNSON IS A STRAIGHT-TALKING, NO-BULLSH*T coach and a person of great sensitivity and understanding. He has spent nearly ten years as a professional grower and twenty-five years as a sales, customer service, and people expert. He is uniquely qualified to lead you and your employees to great success in any aspect of the business. Todd created Weedonomics as an operating system with three pillars: People, Systems, and Products. It includes ongoing support tools, live coaching, and technological advantages that track and ensure you follow proven systems that work.

DON'T YOU WORRY 'BOUT A THING

STEVIE WONDER

Take the Next Step

THIS BOOK MAY BE ALL YOU NEED TO BE ON YOUR WAY to creating a new future in the cannabis industry. I hope you know how great this can be for you. The Weedonomics network will always be here, and you can tap into it anytime in the future.

You may read this book and glean life insights and inspiration, yet not do anything in the cannabis industry, at least not yet. If that's you, consider reaching out to us because we can help you see a path for yourself that you can't see yet. We'll be here when you are ready.

Hopefully, most of you will fully understand that this is the opportunity of a lifetime, and you'll want to move forward with expertise and a new view on life. You know this industry includes a lot of variables, and our Weedonomics coaching and guidance will make all the difference. Remember that you want to start with a great plan, people, systems, and products. That is the key to your successful future. You currently may have a business and need assistance with an operation that is already up and running. We can help with that too.

The Weedonomics system can guide you on these topics, and more:

- Personal Development Coaching
- Strategy Planning
- Mission Statement and Values Workshop
- Sales Training
- Culture Development Workshop
- Team Building and Creating Team Buy-In
- Leadership Development Workshop
- Compliance
- Real Estate
- Legal
- Accounting
- Contractor Evaluation
- Hiring

I'll give you a quick example of what an expert set of eyes can do for your business. I'll tell you a story that has nothing to do with the cannabis industry.

I have used CarMax a few times, and I've been pleased with the service. They are basically a used car warehouse. What's interesting is that they have no sales system. None. They almost refuse to ask you any questions about why you are there, what you are looking for, what your budget is, and when you want to buy a car. Zero. My conclusion is that CarMax is so afraid of seeming like a traditional dealership, which is typically known for high-pressure people and berating sales tactics, that to overcome that, they don't do anything. Remember from back in the sales chapter that people don't mind being sold on something if they are treated well and engaged emotionally. I could set up a simple and easy-feeling sales system so the CarMax people could engage with their customers in a meaningful way. I'm certain that not only are they leaving money on the table, but they are also allowing their customers to drive away not feeling as good as they could about their purchase. An expert set of eyes – from the outside – can make an immense difference in your results.

THE NEXT WEEDONOMICS BOOK: THE GROWING SYSTEM

One of the most important parts of this industry is the growing side of the business. Of course without it, the rest of the industry wouldn't exist. My second book, coming out soon, is titled: *Weedonomics Grow Pro*. It contains every step in the process that you need to follow in order to grow like a pro. I have spent nearly ten years growing marijuana in soil and hydro, and I share the advantages to each in exact detail. I also share a step-by-step process for the grow space, lighting, ventilation, temperature, nutrients, cloning, harvesting … and so much more. My growing system is in the patent process right now to be used under license and for turnkey franchise opportunities in the future. These books go together as two distinct hemispheres exist in this business: the people/office side and the grow/product side. It's just like your brain: the two distinct hemispheres need each other and work perfectly together.

LET IT BE

THE BEATLES

Manufactured by Amazon.ca
Bolton, ON